YOU AND PRESCHOOLERS

YOU
AND
PRESCHOOLERS

by
Elsiebeth McDaniel
and
Lawrence O. Richards

MOODY PRESS
CHICAGO

Library of Congress Cataloging in Publication Data
McDaniel, Elsiebeth.
    You and preschoolers.

    1. Religious education of preschool children.
I. Richards, Lawrence O., joint author. II. Title.
BV1475.8.M3   268'.432   74-15353
ISBN 0-8024-9834-5

Second Printing, 1977

Contents

straight for parents

1

Why Bother?

"Permit the children to come to Me. Do not hinder them, for to their kind belongs the kingdom of God. I assure you, whoever fails to receive the kingdom of God like a little child, will not enter it at all" (Mk 10:14-15, New Berkeley).

Why bother to teach preschoolers? It is a bother, you know! All the visual aids to be collected! The patience it takes to work with two- and three-year-olds! And can they really learn much?

Some adults believe that preschool years are play years, waste years, years of waiting until the action really starts. Unfortunately, too many parents agree with these adults, believing that if children are warm, loved, and fed, all is well. But the first six years of life are reality just as are all of the years after six. We cannot delay development of the muscular or nervous system. Neither can we believe that nothing happens in spiritual matters till after the age of six.

If we believe we can waste these first six years by doing no spiritual teaching, we are like the amateur gardener who decided that vegetables and flowers would appear in his uncared for plot of ground without his help. Children will not develop love for God unless concerned adults tell them about Him. We know that all living things—plant or animal—change. Children change as they mature physically. Surely part of their changing and developing must be in spiritual growth. We cannot—we must not—fail to see that young children develop spiritually.

Professor Arthur Jensen, School of Education, University of California, says, "Our present knowledge of the development of learning abilities indicates that the preschool years are the most important years of learning in a child's life. A tremendous amount of learning takes place during these years, and this learning is the foundation for all future learning."[1]

Christian teaching cannot be neglected until a child is four or five. If it is, there is permanent loss. It is impossible to go back and give a child experiences he has missed. We can demonstrate this fact with physical development and ac-

1. Arthur R. Jensen, "Learning in the Preschool Years," in *The Young Child,* ed. Willard W. Hartup and Nancy L. Smothergill (Washington, D.C.: National Association for the Education of Young Children), p. 125.

complishment. Some young children do not have tricycles; nor are they given bicycles when they become older. If a boy of twelve receives a bicycle for his birthday, what type is it likely to be? Probably a three-speed or possibly a ten-speed. The boy will learn to ride and enjoy it, but he will never know a three-year-old's pleasure in the exciting experience of riding a tricycle as fast as he can. The twelve-year-old will never know the fun of tying a wagon or string of cars to the back of his trike and proudly driving his "train" along the sidewalk.

If spiritual experiences are missed, they cannot be provided at another time. When a child misses out on spiritual teaching during his early years, we must reach him where he is when his first encounter with spiritual truth takes place. At twelve, a child should not be afraid of the dark. He has overcome some other fears because he no longer feels small and insignificant in a world of towering adults. However, because he is twelve, his mind and his years of experience will not enable him to discover the comfort and security of Jesus' love in a two- or three-year-old way.

Priscilla was afraid. She was all alone in the dark bedroom; everyone else was downstairs. She began to sing a Sunday school song, "Jesus Is with Me All Through the Night."

As Priscilla related the incident the next Sunday, we realized that the Lord Jesus had really helped her to fall asleep peacefully. If Priscilla's parents had not seen the advantages of spiritual teaching at home and in Sunday school, she could not have known the good and happy feeling a young child has when he depends on the Lord for his needs.

Another true story will help emphasize the importance of early spiritual training. Ten-month-old David's mother began having a quiet time with him each afternoon before his nap. Mother did not pray long prayers, but she did sing a hymn and held David's hands while she prayed briefly. By the time David was fifteen months old, he was bowing his head in a good imitation of his mother. Then, before he was two, David volunteered to talk to God and made up his own sentence prayers.

Why did God send His Son as a baby when the Saviour could have come as a man? Is Christ's development significant for us? If the Bible relates in Luke 2:52 that the boy Jesus developed physically, mentally, and spiritually, is it not realistic to believe that this is the pattern God wants for all boys and girls?

The Bible verse at the beginning of this chapter states that Jesus invited children to come to Him. His words are more important than anything else anyone has ever said about children. Evangelically, Jesus recognized that young children need to come to Him. Psychologically, the words emphasize that everyone needs to experience the Lord's love. Socially, His words indicate that all children are equal in being accepted by the Lord. We do not know the ages of the children who came to Jesus on that day long ago, but because He took some of them in His arms, we know they were not all teenagers or even tens and twelves. There were some young children, toddlers, and runabouts of preschool years.

Too many people worry about the teen years without realizing that all the years before thirteen help to make a child what he is. Often the so-called rebellion of a teenager is only the small child inside the big one still seeking love and acceptance. If a child has a happy, confident time during his preschool and later childhood years, he will undoubtedly be a better adjusted teenager. However, when a young child faces frustration and insecurity in his growing up years, he may still be seeking acceptance, confidence, love, and security as a teenager. Surely some teens rebel because they have never felt loved and accepted. No one has ever helped them to feel "big" and competent as young children.

Some educators also believe that the negative teen is very much like the two-year-old with his insistent no. The two-year-old is testing his authority, his ability to make some choices, and to move at his own pace. When a two-year-old says no, he may also mean, "Don't rush me," or, "Let me wait a minute," or, "I will, but not now." Is it possible that if we deal less emotionally and vigorously with the *nos* of teens, we can better enlist their cooperation? There are no easy solutions to teenage problems, but the two ideas in these paragraphs should be considered.

When you become aware of preschoolers and their needs, you become aware of your opportunity and responsibility. Preschoolers are among the persons to whom the church ministers. And they are everywhere—in high-rise apartments, along back roads, in the city ghettos, and throughout suburbia. These little people are developing into adults. As preschoolers they are clay, but clay hardens after it has been molded or left in its original state.

Why bother to teach preschoolers? Because the roots of most of the social evils of our day are attributed to what happened in early childhood. Dr. James Hymes, an authority on early childhood development, says, "If any years have a very special importance it is those long years before school begins, way back in early childhood. Those baby years when youngsters are just getting their initial impression of this world."[2]

The kind of emotional disturbance that is likely to lead to violent behavior has its roots in early childhood. Self-control, tolerance, cheerfulness, and acceptance of others all develop in an atmosphere where children receive adequate care, enough supervision, guidance, and love. Early emotional deprivation and an atmosphere filled with unhealthy adult attitudes accounts for most of the violent people in today's society.

Child psychologists agree that the early years are the most formative period of life, that the child's future is determined largely by these early influences. The child's outlook on life,

---

2. James L. Hymes, *Understanding Your Child* (Englewood Cliffs, N.J.: Prentice-Hall, 1952), p. 184.

his estimate of true values, and his religious attitudes are all influenced during the first few years of life. The people who influence him and shape his attitudes are, first of all, his parents. Next, he is influenced by other significant adults who enter his life. Sunday school teachers, children's workers, nursery school and kindergarten teachers are certainly among these significant adults.

Preschool years are in reality the longest period when a child will believe anything, is most dependent, is learning the most, and is also undergoing rapid physical and mental development. These are the years when a child is gaining control over his environment primarily through his senses and is trying to integrate and assimilate what he sees, hears, feels, and even tastes. Is it important for Christian adults to help guide the child in these experiences? During these believing years, a child is trying to fit pieces together and understand the world in which he lives. How very important it is for him to find the Creator and Sustainer of the things that arouse his curiosity and wonder! A young child marvels at the travels of a dandelion seed, the soft fur of a kitten, and a duck's ability to dive. As the young child grows in appreciation of God and all He has made, he may respond in the words of one four-year-old, "Isn't God clever?"

If you are to teach preschoolers, you must have a good Sunday school curriculum that takes into account the growth of children, not only physical, but mental and spiritual. Only in the last twenty-five to thirty years has there been much concern in the church about preschoolers. Even so, many of the early programs for nursery children were very similar to secular kindergartens. Teachers did not have biblical curriculums, and so they patterned their teaching after the public kindergarten, injecting a few Bible verses "to keep the lessons spiritual." However, we now know that children under six are ready for many spiritual truths (see chap. 4).

Today, Christian education recognizes the growth patterns of young children. Through recognizing normal development, we are better prepared to teach the whole child and to pace the Sunday school program to his needs and abilities. As Agnes Snyder says, in speaking of secular education,

> A good program for children takes into account the paces at which children grow. It takes time for children to develop muscular coordination to enjoy instead of to strain. To build up a wealth of experiences through the senses and muscles before verbalizing adult concepts. Time to pass naturally from early absorption in self into gradually widening circles of human interest; time for children to feel with all the abundance of early childhood emotion and to move slowly into finer gradations of feeling; time for children to think and wonder.[3]

In teaching a preschooler spiritual truths, you must: (1) help a child find meaning where he is right now; (2) lay foundations for his conversion when he reaches the age of accountability; and (3) provide a foundation for his continuing growth and service as a Christian. In teaching preschoolers, you show God's love and how He expects His people to live. A few children may be able to understand salvation and receive Christ as Saviour. (See chap. 4 for a detailed discussion of salvation and conversion.) However, many preschoolers need more time to realize their need of a Saviour.

Should you become unduly concerned about the age of accountability? Is every child accountable at the same age? Is every four-year-old exhibiting the same manual dexterity? Are all five-year-old boys the same height? Of course, you are deeply concerned about teaching children to respond to God as they are ready. By teaching how God expects His people to obey Him and to treat others, you are also explaining a standard which, sooner or later, thinking boys and girls will realize they cannot attain; they will need God's help. If you did not teach the standards of Christian behavior, it is

---

3. Agnes Snyder, "The Roots of Growth," *Childhood Education*, October 1973, p. 11.

possible that children would never know what God expects of them or how He has provided for their salvation. If the love of God is reality, then it is part of a meaningful life. Preschoolers need to be introduced to this life in ways they can understand. If life is worthless without Jesus, then why not teach preschoolers something about life with Jesus?

Before a child becomes a Christian, you are helping him learn what is the standard of behavior acceptable to God. This process begins even before a child is old enough to know what it means to receive Jesus Christ as Saviour. When you teach young children God's truth, you are preparing the soil into which the seed, the Word of God, may take root and grow. The child who attends Sunday school during his early years—and particularly a child from a Christian home—is ready sooner to be led by the Holy Spirit to believe that Jesus loves him, is his Friend, and wants the child's love in return.

Through your teaching and the example of other Christians, the young child sees ways of thinking and acting in accordance with God's Word. By observing the actions of adults around him, the little child begins to recognize sharing, helping, being kind, and other expressions of love as patterns of life for those who love Jesus.

A child who receives scriptural teaching develops a biblical awareness of the world in which he lives. He feels that his life and his world of people and experiences are all a part of God's loving plan and care for him. If the young child can early believe in God and count on His unconditional love for him as a person of worth, he can begin to cope with the experiences of life. He feels secure in the reality of God's unchanging love.

You cannot make a child into a Christian by trying to get his behavior to conform to Bible standards. However, a young child who is familiar with what God's Word teaches is better prepared to become a Christian.

Why bother to teach preschoolers? Because God says,

"Train up a child," and we who are His older children want to obey.

REACT

1. In your own experience, what makes teaching preschoolers important?
2. Very early in life, a child has his first confrontation with reality. He decides to keep his guard up, or he decides to trust people. How can you influence his choice?
3. Are you aware that young children have their moments of depression as well as feelings that life is good? What are some factors that cause these feelings in young children?

ACT

1. Children under six can be infuriating if you don't understand them. Want to make your work with them easier? Then get to know these people, and you will make your own life more peaceful and your teaching more meaningful. Decide to read this book and apply its principles to your own teaching.
2. If you are not teaching, think about the responsibility of working with young children. If you accept a teaching assignment, you must take on the responsibility 100 percent. Teaching young children, perhaps even more than an older age, means you must be there! You cannot be present one week and gone the next without an important reason. When are you justified in being absent?
3. The teacher of young children recognizes that his faith, beliefs, and attitudes become part of the children he teaches. Are you willing to have your beliefs become part of a child's life? Are there things you want to change?

4. Remember, you do not *make* children respond to God, but sufficient Bible teaching, as directed by the Holy Spirit, helps a child *want* to respond to God. Are you ready for God to share His work with you?

2

How Do You Qualify?

"As ye have therefore received Christ Jesus the Lord, so walk ye in him: Rooted and built up in him, and stablished in the faith, as ye have been taught, abounding therein with thanksgiving" (Col 2:6-7).

"Anyone can teach young children! After all, they are easily amused," someone tells you. How simply that person equates amusing children with teaching them! This person confuses quiet children with learning children; the two are not always the same.

If someone should ask you to teach preschoolers, prefacing the request with remarks about how easy it will be because preschoolers can't learn much, would you agree? Not if you have read and believed chapter 1! You now realize and would say that those under six are some of the most important people anyone can ever teach.

Any man or woman who decides to teach preschoolers realizes that, first of all, he or she must have a vital relationship with Jesus Christ. God has said, "That ye might walk worthy of the Lord unto all pleasing, being fruitful in every good work, and increasing in the knowledge of God" (Col 1:10). This Bible verse and the one at the beginning of the chapter offer an excellent description of a teacher—the believer who walks with God, being built up in Him, and increasing in the knowledge of the Lord.

A teacher must know the Lord intimately, believing in Him as personal Saviour and growing in the knowledge of Him. To become a teacher should mean a calling from God and a dedication to Him for a special service. And when Christians teach because they love the Lord Jesus, that love is bound to show in love for others. We become persons who teach because we care about the people we teach—little children—and we care for them as individuals.

This chapter will help you discover qualities a preschool teacher needs to teach the children described in chapter 3. Chapters 4 and 5 will tell you what preschoolers can learn and that they learn best through educational or structured play. The room, the materials, and the furniture are all part of the learning environment, but they are not the most important factor. You, the teacher, are the key to successful teaching and learning in the preschool departments of your Sunday school.

Because the teacher is the key to success, churches should want the very best qualified people. You, teacher, are the person who will reflect the Lord Jesus and His love for children under six.

> You, yourself, teacher, are the voice through whom God speaks the name of a child as He spoke the name of Samuel long ago; and the day will come when the child will recognize the voice as the Lord's, and will answer, 'Speak, Lord, for Thy servant heareth.' It is your hand holding the child's which leads him gently in the paths of righteousness until he recognizes that over your hand is the hand of Christ, which was wounded for him.[1]

What makes a good preschool teacher? A number of Christian educators have developed lists of commandments for teachers. Most of these lists are helpful because the same ideas come up again and again, facts that help identify the qualifications of a good preschool teacher. In addition to knowing the Lord Jesus, Marion Lawrance says, "A teacher must be a real man or woman." Decide for yourself what this early Christian educator meant, but I believe that he was saying a teacher should be the highest and best example that any man or woman can be. Someone has said that throughout the years men have been looking for better methods but God has been looking for better men and women.

The preschool teacher must believe in the Book he teaches and grow in his knowledge of it. He should read the Book and live it. The preschool lessons may contribute little additional Bible knowledge, so the teacher must make study a personal habit.

The best preschool teacher has genuine love for people. His love will be felt by both children and parents. The

---

1. Lois E. LeBar, *Children in the Bible School* (Old Tappan, N.J.: Revell, 1952), p. 32.

teacher will be sensitive to the needs of young children, remembering that during the church session, he is a substitute parent when there are times to rub or kiss away an imagined or real hurt. The teacher knows when the problem of the moment demands a story or when to pray for a special need mentioned by a child. He knows when it is time to suggest a spontaneous activity because it fits the mood.

The teacher must believe in prayer, because he must pray for himself and for those he teaches. Martin Luther is credited with a thought that no Christian should forget. Someone came across this statement in his papers, "I am so busy with so many things to attend to that I must spend at least three hours in prayer every day." Unfortunately today's Christians often reverse this thought to mean, "Lord, when I have time and there is less to do, I'll pray more."

A preschool teacher must be willing to work and learn, because there will always be more to know about children. We are teaching living persons, and they will change; their problems will change. A preschool teacher will enjoy children for what they are. The Bible says no one can grow taller by taking thought to it, nor is it likely that any preschool teacher can change a two-year-old into a ten-year-old or a four-year-old into a fourteen-year-old. Teachers of young children must accept the children where they are and enjoy them and their activities.

Preschool teachers may need to be champions of a cause as yet unrecognized by the church. A walk through many of our churches would indicate that the average church is not thinking of young children. Many times the small children are placed in undesirable rooms, and the best rooms are reserved for the adults "who have earned them." Yes, adults are deserving of good facilities, but adults can give and allocate money for better facilities. Preschoolers cannot. Then, too, most adults are attending church because they believe what the church teaches. Preschoolers, on the other hand, are in the process of deciding what to believe. If the room and its furnishings will lead young children to the Saviour more quickly, let's provide that room. The young child is looking for beauty and for a feeling of being loved. Will he find them in your church?

A preschool teacher must be ready to reach children through being childlike himself. What does this mean? Walk into the typical preschool Sunday school room. Can you tell what the children would like or what would be unattractive to them? Can you see the surroundings as helping or hindering a lesson? How would you like to bend your head back and look about twelve feet up to see the picture a teacher holds? This is an exaggeration, of course, but when a tall adult stands, holding a picture under his chin and looking down at the little people seated below his knees, the effect is the same.

If a teacher is childlike, he will be able to see the world through a child's eyes, to think as a child, to see the joy and excitement of life; he will have some understanding of the importance of play; he will also try to think concretely and literally, instead of using abstract thoughts and figurative or symbolic language. A childlike teacher will realize how much each child needs a teacher. He will also realize that he must understand his role as teacher.

The attitude of the teacher is the most important factor in the discipline of preschoolers. This is not a plea for permissiveness nor for an authoritarian attitude. It is, instead, a request for a normal, consistent, realistic attitude toward preschoolers and their problems. Discipline must develop self-control, not merely elicit behavior pleasing to the teacher. In guiding young children, you will recognize that they need a great deal of individual attention and are likely to become overstimulated when the group becomes too large or the activities too exciting. Two-year-olds enjoy being with six to eight other children; three-year-olds with about ten other preschoolers; and four- and five-year-olds should not be in groups of more than twenty to twenty-five children.

Discipline will surely include setting the example. Pre-schoolers need this kind of help for motivation and because they sometimes do not know what they are to do. Are you ready to pick up fifty-four blocks; to mend and straighten books; to clean tables; to pick up odd bits of paper and rearrange crayons and scissors; to live with children in ways that show them your love for the Lord? This is all part of the teaching-learning ministry with preschoolers.

Remember that discipline is not just for the child who flagrantly breaks the rules and squeezes you into a corner where you must do something. Discipline and punishment should not be considered synonymous. Try to think of discipline as a means of helping children govern their own behavior in ways which are good for them and good for others. Any limits you set should be realistic and should be for the good of the children. "We don't let children hurt each other." "We don't want children to take all of the blocks when other children need some to play with too." "We don't let people throw puzzle pieces around so they are lost. Then no one else can play with the puzzle." "We don't let children tear books so that other children can't read them." This type of approach is sensible to preschoolers. They can see the value of limits such as these, realizing that they too will benefit from these regulations. Such brief explanations are more effective than merely saying, "You mustn't grab all the blocks!" "You can't play with the puzzles if you throw the pieces." Set the rule that unacceptable behavior denies a child some of the materials, but be sure your explanation is brief and complete enough to help him understand the situation.

Do you realize that if you commend a child when he is doing well, it will be easier to redirect his future wrong actions? Teachers who zero in on a child only when he is misbehaving are not helping that child to develop as a whole person. Every child needs to like himself, to feel wanted and worthy. However, if your personal comments come only when the child is misbehaving, you are doing him a disservice. The child who is told when he does something well learns to accept himself, is eager to grow and develop, and can enjoy others. Children are constantly working with attitudes toward themselves and others, and teachers must help them. When four-year-old Tom made the rounds one Sunday morning asking other boys, "Do you like me?", he was trying to discover how others felt about him.

In setting up limits, you may sometimes say, "You can't do finger painting today, but you can work with clay." When you deny some activity or object, you will find it helpful to you and the child if you suggest an alternative. Respect a child as a person so that he will come to respect himself. Be trustworthy and accept the child's need for dependence on you without making him feel "little" or inferior.

How do you treat parents in the preschool department? They should always be welcome visitors. However, you will want to recommend that they observe, not participate. Tell parents of new children not to sneak out of the room unobserved by their child. Imagine how you would feel if your source of security suddenly disappeared! It is much better for Mother or Father to say ahead of time, "After a while I may go to my class, but my coat (or some other object) will be here on the chair. I'll get it when I come back for you."

Do not give children more responsibility than they can handle. It is ridiculous to expect preschoolers to put all materials away on their own. The same is true of turning threes and fours out into the hall to get drinks. Young children want an adult around who knows his way and who will help them behave as they should.

Learning to teach young children is a continuing process. You will never know all that there is to know. Your first requisite is a sincere love for the Lord. Next, you should love little children. Then as you continue to study children, materials, and methods, remember the following simple rules.

1. Put safety first. This rule will help you consider the health and welfare of every child. You will be watchful of equipment as well as experiences, such as leaning from an open window or stepping out onto the fire escape.
2. Always speak to individual children by name. Speak quietly and clearly, in positive rather than negative terms. You may say, "Bobby, we use the crayons on paper," instead of "Children, don't use the crayons on the wall." Preschoolers will respond better to personal recognition; in fact, many may not "hear" until you use their names. Because preschoolers are so unaware in a play situation, sometimes you will have to touch a child to gain his attention.
3. When you are making a suggestion to redirect a child's activity, speak and act as though you expected it to be carried out. Perhaps some two-year-olds are throwing blocks. Touch the child or children lightly on arm or shoulder, saying, "Blocks are for building." Then pile a few blocks yourself, inviting the children to join you.
4. Try to stop trouble before it starts. When you see a two-year-old preparing to take a plaything from another child, immediately offer a similar plaything or substitute one which might serve the purpose. You may soon find your twos bargaining among themselves in a more peaceful fashion.
5. Discriminate between situations in which a child has a choice, and ones in which routines must be carried out.
6. In all your relationships be friendly, interested, and understanding.

Haim Ginott says, "A teacher is a concerned human being first and always. As a teacher he acts appropriately in stressful situations. He shows grace under pressure. He responds insightfully. He does not react impulsively."[2] Do you agree?

---

2. Haim Ginott, *Teacher and Child* (New York: Macmillan, 1972), p. 57.

Teachers of preschoolers must have good physical health. You cannot teach and move and be vibrant if you are not feeling well. Endless questions from children, crises in dealing with physical disturbances or hurt feelings, and movement in many activities all demand a measure of good health.

Teachers in a preschool department must develop a team attitude. With older children, the individual teacher may be the star performer, but young children need a team of teachers. Teachers should take turns in guiding the activities. Even though there are only a half-dozen children in the department, teaching and learning will be more effective if responsibilities are shared by more than one teacher.

Teachers of young children should be regular in attendance, giving the children a feeling of security because the same adults are waiting for them each week. Regularity is in first place, but punctuality cannot be divorced from it. Teachers must come on time in order to be unhurried, to greet the first child, and to have the room and materials ready. Primaries and juniors can, if necessary, help set up the room and activities, but preschoolers cannot. Materials must be ready for preschoolers. Reading books must be displayed attractively, materials laid out for art activities, learning centers arranged for use, and a record player or flannelboard ready and waiting. You will want children to help whenever they can, but during preschool years, their interest in helping will be fleeting and their abilities limited.

Early-childhood teachers recognize that they must create the environment for spiritual learning. They will be prepared to structure learning experiences, but they will also be flexible enough to change according to pupil needs and teachable moments.

"Know what? We have a new puppy," says one of your preschoolers just as you are ready to tell the Bible story. What do you do? First, if at all possible, you encourage preschoolers to talk when they first come into Sunday school. However, if a child interrupts in this way, you can make him feel happy by recognizing his contribution and also continuing the story by saying, "How happy you must be to have a new puppy!", or, "We're glad you have a puppy, Dan!" Then continue with the Bible story. You have not asked a question which would demand more conversation. You did not ask other children how they felt and thus started many children to thinking about dogs. You recognized the child's feelings, but continued with your lesson.

Do you have a happy face? A preschool teacher needs to wear one. Good teachers lead children to learn, and to learn with joy.

Do you become excited when you realize that a young child is discovering the reality of God's love? Perhaps someone asks prayer for his father or mentions a weekday experience that enables you to see spiritual truth linked to life.

You must pray and expect that the Holy Spirit will work through you to cause the Word to take root in individual lives. Good teachers are not born but are made through their efforts and through the work of the Lord Jesus in their lives. You, teacher, can never do the Lord's work in the hearts of your pupils, but you can grow in your knowledge of the Lord, His Word, and your pupils. You can pray for each child, the stubborn and misbehaving, the unloved and perverse. You can prepare to the best of your ability and then depend on God to use you!

REACT

1. It has been said that to make God real to a young child, we must surround him with people to whom God is real. Why is this true?
2. "The child who identifies with his teacher through affection, admiration, and submissiveness will 'take unto himself' not only what the teacher believes and teaches but

also what he is and does."[3] This statement is made about all teachers. What part of it do you accept for preschool teachers?

ACT

1. Make a list of the qualifications given in this chapter. Give yourself a score, varying from excellent (1) to poor (5) on each qualification.
2. Can you grow in your relationship to the Lord Jesus? Will you?

---

3. A. H. Jahsmann, *How You Too Can Teach* (St. Louis: Concordia, 1963), p. 19.

3

Who Are the Preschoolers?

Preschoolers are motion and sound! They are wigglers and questioners. They speak with their bodies as well as with their tongues. They are curious, questioning, and active. Every one of them is unique from every other preschooler! Each one insists on "being me."

Preschoolers are children between the ages of two and five—little people who want to feel big. They have very special spiritual needs that you can help to meet. What needs preschoolers have and what Bible truths they can understand are discussed fully in chapter 4; the present chapter will describe preschoolers and make some generalizations about their development.

Every preschooler has ability to learn about God and to grow in spiritual understanding. How he grows depends on how you teach and what you understand about his particular characteristics. What preschoolers can learn and how you will teach are important subjects—so important that they deserve special chapters in this book. This chapter focuses on the development of preschoolers, describing certain characteristics of each year of development. Sometimes every month makes a big difference in the life of a young child.

Some things are the same about most preschoolers, but many things are not the same! Therefore, do not combine all preschoolers, two through five, in one group and expect to teach them efficiently. Preschoolers learn more in small groups: five or six in a group is best for two- and three-year-olds; and *never* more than twenty to twenty-five in a group of four- and five-year-olds. (Teaching methods and learning groups will be explained in later chapters.)

Some preschoolers look bigger than others of the same age. When this is the case, teachers are tempted to think that "big" children should know more and be more responsible. Or adults may make another mistake by thinking that the "small" preschooler is exceptional for his age. But all preschoolers, regardless of age, are somewhere in the process of growing from "me" to "we" as they see the example of adults and respond to their teaching. All children are interested in "becoming," wanting to feel "big" and believing that they can learn and do, just as God Himself intended.

Preschoolers have hungry senses. They want to see,

touch, hear, smell, push, pull, smash, move, and even taste. These young children need to move; they *cannot* be still for a long time. Adults should not try to equate being *still* with being *good*, for preschoolers are limited in the length of time they can remain quiet. Muscles scream to move! Two-year-olds seem to need constant activity, but five-year-olds can control their need to move and be quiet as long as they are really interested. When teachers recognize preschoolers' need to move, they plan programs to alternate between quiet and active times. An active time provides for bodily movement, and a quiet time is a listening time.

Not only do preschoolers want to move, but they also want to talk. A young child feels that his talking is more important than yours. He wants his turn even if you have to stop! You should always plan for a time in Sunday school when children can talk; a time early in the hour is better than halfway through the session. You may want to come early to greet individual children, or you may encourage conversation at interest centers, but you *must* plan for conversation with your preschoolers.

During the years from two to five, children make great physical progress. Large muscle coordination improves, but the small muscles do not develop as rapidly or as well. Preschoolers' physical capabilities grow from the first steps of the toddler to the running fast and skipping abilities of five-year-olds. Eye-hand coordination develops during these years. Some preschoolers, especially those who are four and five, may do well at pasting, cutting, threading beads, or performing other intricate work. However, the average preschooler is happiest when he is using his large muscles to clap, stretch, run, bend, and sway.

Preschoolers are curious. They ask limitless questions! "What is it? Why?" they want to know. If you listen carefully, you'll discover that these little people are proficient in finding out why, who, where, when, how, and what. Young children often like to ask the same question over and over, as they retest their knowledge or that of adults. (Of course, questioning can also be a means of getting attention, something all children want and need.)

By all means, encourage preschoolers' curiosity. Praise them for wanting to find out by providing right answers and helping them to discover other answers for themselves. Adults need to be ready to give direction but not to smother the questioner with information. Someone has said, "Don't answer questions the pupils aren't asking." The same philosophy applies in any conversation with preschoolers. An older child resents long explanations when he doesn't need them and may say so, but when preschoolers lose interest, they dart off to something that does attract them.

Depending on his age, a preschooler may be quite adventuresome. Two-year-olds are content to climb for the fun and adventure of climbing, but four- and five-year-olds want to climb the slide in order to come down backward. In play skills, preschoolers move from the block-piling stage of age two to the building of intricate structures designed by fives or fours. Two-year-olds are likely to crayon with long curving strokes, enjoying the brightness of color and the movement of crayon on paper. Five-year-olds, on the other hand, will work carefully to perfect a recognizable drawing.

You should remember that a young child's emotions are very near the surface. Tears may erupt because of loneliness, a lost shoe buckle, competition from another child, or failure to hang onto a favorite toy or possession. The Christian teacher must be careful not to capitalize on emotional response when telling a Bible story or reprimanding unacceptable behavior.

Now that we have described some of the general characteristics of preschoolers, let's look at each age, noting some of the recognizable differences.

Who is two?

We are beginning our study of preschoolers at age two, the

year when children usually begin attending Sunday school. Being two is important, and both church and home need to recognize the two-year-olds who are passing from toddler stage to the runabout age. A child of two is aware of himself. He can understand when an adult says, "Who made Ann? God made Ann!"

A two-year-old may appear to be a very negative person. However, his frequent use of *no* should not be interpreted as mere obstinacy or contrariness. A two-year-old is trying out the word *no* and sometimes means, "Don't rush me. Let me look some more. Wait till I'm ready." Ignore the *no* when possible, or invite the child to change activity. A two-year-old is just at the edge of considering other people, both children or adults. Some two-year-olds will challenge the aggressive behavior of another child, but others will look on helplessly while the aggressive child walks away with a favorite toy.

Play for most two- and three-year-olds is generally parallel play. The term *parallel play* is used to describe children who play *side by side,* either at the same activity, such as using clay or blocks, or who play at different activities, such as pounding a peg block and dressing a doll.

Two-year-olds may be ready to experiment with friendship, offering a toy to another child or responding in some other way, but they really are not ready to share. It is usually better if a teacher offers the second child a substitute toy or activity instead of insisting that the first child give up what he feels is rightfully his. Of course, a teacher will sometimes suggest, "Tommy would like a turn too. Please let him play with your toy after a while."

A two-year-old may still be quite cuddly, or he may be so independent that he does not want to be held or picked up. His vocabulary may be large or small. He has probably learned to feed himself, but he cannot perform such delicate operations as cutting with a knife or stabbing a bite of food with a fork. Recognize his limited skill, and plan handwork activities that do not tire and frustrate him.

Two-year-olds like routine. If they are accustomed to finding things in a certain place, they can learn to put them back again. Do not hesitate to expect two-year-olds to help put toys away. However, do not make cleanup time such a chore that the children become resentful and fussy. Conversation or a song helps them join you and others in putting things away. A song one nursery teacher uses is repetition of the same phrase, "I'm helping, I'm helping because I love Jesus." Sometimes she varies it to say, "I'm picking up scraps (or blocks or toys) because I love Jesus."

Who is three?

A three-year-old is still developing large muscle control, but he is sure on his feet. He plays hard and tires easily. If he is interested, he pays attention, but once you have lost his interest, you have lost him. Three-year-olds are not too different from two-year-olds in darting from one activity to another. That is why interest centers are important in the nursery department. Children at age three are more flexible than they were at two; they respond to your suggestions and your plans for structured play. However, both twos and threes are essentially very egocentric.

A child of three is less negative than the two-year-old. This is partly because he is in better command of himself and his environment; he knows his way around. Three-year-olds will play together in a limited way, but they still enjoy playing alone. Adults will find three-year-olds more ready to talk to them and to other children because they have a larger vocabulary and feel more comfortable about the nursery activities. Do not lose your opportunities for conversation. Be sure to listen as much or more than you talk. When you do have something to say, try to guide the conversation meaningfully, choosing words to help children learn. If a child comments about his new shoes, you may say, "They're pretty." However, you could make your conversation mean more by responding, "Aren't they pretty? Wasn't it good of Daddy (or Mother) to buy them for you? Have you thanked God for your new shoes?"

A three-year-old is quite capable of bargaining for what he wants. A two-year-old may grab a toy, but a three-year-old will try substituting another toy or will invite the second child to share by telling what he will do with it. Brent's suggestion to Keith illustrates this idea. Keith brought a small toy motorcycle to the nursery department. Brent wanted to play with it too. Here is the conversation that gave Brent a turn.

"What's that?" asked Brent, though he knew the answer.

"My motorcycle," replied Keith.

"I could make it go fast. Want to see?" offered Brent.

Brent raced the motorcycle across the room and then carefully returned it to Keith, saying, "See how fast I did it?"

Preschoolers like to feel big by helping. Three-year-olds are usually ready to be helpers as long as an adult does not insist a job always be finished or done exactly according to adult standards. Let three-year-olds do what they can; do not kill their desire to help by requiring too much of them.

Who is four?

Four is a stormy age, but much less physical than two or three. Two- and three-year-olds hit with their fists, and sometimes they kick and bite. Four- and five-year-olds are more likely to use words or actions that show disregard and disapproval.

Betty had a birthday. At Sunday school, Scott was invited to help her blow out the candles on the artificial birthday cake, but Todd rushed to the front of the room, hoping to blow out candles too. The teacher sent Todd back to his chair. Four-year-old Todd did not cry, but when Scott sat down again, Todd tried spitting at him. Todd kept up this effort to condemn Scott by spitting and blowing, till a teacher forcibly moved him to another chair.

Four-year-olds begin to be fascinated by words. They like the sound of new words and are delighted when they make up "silly" words of their own. At four, perhaps even earlier, many children invent imaginary playmates who serve them well. On more than one occasion, Jackie described her imaginary friend, Judy, so vividly that a well-meaning but unknowing hostess sent home another portion of birthday treats "for Judy."

The four-year-old may seem big and grown up, but he is not. He still needs adult help and direction. Four-year-olds respond well to adults because they are beginning to recognize that both children and adults have feelings. Many children of four are ready to play happily with another child, often selecting a "best" friend of the same sex.

Four-year-olds are adventuresome. They enjoy trying more things by themselves—both physical and mental endeavors. James Hymes describes growing in preschool years when he says, "During all the years under six, children devise more and more ways to use their bodies freely and with increasing skill."[1]

Who is five?

Five is a comfortable age, not nearly as stormy and boisterous as four. A child of five has good control of his body. His large muscles are much better developed, but he still has difficulty with the small muscles that control his fingers and hands. Five-year-olds should use large brushes and crayons in their art activities. They have passed the stage of merely

---

1. James L. Hymes, Jr., *The Child Under Six*, p. 108.

smearing or dabbing with art materials and are working purposefully, knowing what they want to achieve. Five-year-olds will work for twenty minutes or longer at an activity that really interests them.

Five-year-olds usually know how to take turns and respect other people's belongings. According to the direction provided by adults, they are learning right from wrong and can recognize in many situations what they should do. These children love stories, but they like best the stories that teach something new about places, persons, or interesting things.

Between the ages of two to six, most children gain from 500 to 600 new words a year. Therefore, the five-year-old may have a vocabulary of 3000 words, but you must still be sure that he understands the meaning or meanings of words. Too many classic stories are told of preschoolers who misunderstood. For example, did the "pilot" who judged Jesus also fly a plane? Was Abraham's tent like the one a child's family bought from Sears? A five-year-old is still thinking very literally and concretely. He is no more ready for symbolism than he was at three or four.

Five-year-olds are conformists, doing what they see other children or adults do. Though perhaps further along in growing unselfish, moving from the "me" to the "we" viewpoint, a child of five is still very self-centered. However, he is more aware of others and is growing in friendliness and concern. Because he can play with others and enjoys it, he will feel left out if not included in group activities. A two-year-old may wander off when he does not feel part of a group, but a five-year-old will stand alone and suffer the terrible pangs of loneliness and insecurity.

Five-year-olds are still physically active and rely on their senses to help them learn. However, these preschoolers will ask more thoughtful questions and will want to talk longer and oftener when they gain an adult's attention. Five-year-olds are on the brink of the wonderful world of reading books. They are almost ready to stop being preschoolers and to become "big" first graders.

Do not be tricked by this artificial division made by some adults. Six-year-olds still enjoy make-believe and running and shouting. They do not suddenly become quiet and lose their love and need of physical activity. No, six is just the next year when children still grow in feeling big and independent. Six-year-olds are different in some ways from five-year-olds, but do not expect that when a five-year-old leaves your Sunday school department he changes overnight into a really big boy or girl. If you have been watching individuals and trying to "learn" your children, you have seen your five-year-olds becoming more and more like six throughout the year.

Do you really know?

Now you have some general ideas about children during their preschool years. But do you know each child individually? Can you honestly say you are aware of individual feelings? When have you been interested enough to really listen? Who among your group is shy and needs to be drawn out of his or her timidity?

How well do you know the homes of your children? Whose grandfather is sick? Who vacations in a camper or tent? What children compete for attention with older brothers and sisters? Who is an only child and may not identify when you talk about brothers and sisters? What child in your group feels displaced because a new baby requires all of Mother's attention?

It is not enough to know generalities. Use the characteristics given in this book as a good beginning to help you concentrate on knowing each child. Take time to listen to your children because through listening, you will discover needs. Then you will begin to see your children as distinct individuals. You will pray more specifically and prepare with enthusiasm because you know Johnny, Jenny, Sam, and all the others.

REACT

1. What is the single most important characteristic of preschoolers? Do you agree it is their need to move and develop through their senses?
2. Think of a preschooler you know. Can you see the "me" stage in his attitudes? When do you see his awareness of "we"?

ACT

1. If you are teaching preschoolers, what activities do you provide to take care of the need to move?
2. When do you have quiet times in your program?
3. Will you resolve to read on in this book in order to become a more effective teacher? Does your resolve include learning to tell stories meaningfully, not merely to arouse emotions?

4

What Can They Learn?

> "And that from a child thou hast known the holy scriptures, which are able to make thee wise unto salvation through faith which is in Christ Jesus" (2 Ti 3:15).

"Can a little child really learn about God?" asks someone who has never worked with little children. The questioner has never read a book on early childhood development and does not understand the capacities of little children. He tends to excuse the lack of spiritual objectives in a program for young children.

Experience, the Word of God, and young children themselves all testify to the value of early instruction in spiritual truth. Young children can learn to know God, to love Jesus, to respect the Bible, and to grow in love toward others. It is during the early years that lifelong attitudes are formed. These are foundational years and must be carefully built because it should not be necessary to remove any inferior material from the foundation laid in early years. Spiritual truth learned at two, three, four, and five should be held true for life. We should never have to help a child unlearn spiritual "truth." If teachers oversimplify truth or teach error because they believe it is more understandable, God will hold them accountable.

Dr. Anna Mow, widely recognized for her work with early childhood education, says, "A child's experience of God is real. It is as real as the love in his life. The imperfection or immaturity of his image of God is never a hindrance to him unless the image was created by a loved adult. Whenever he realizes that some image he formed himself is wrong or inadequate, it is easily sloughed off by the new idea that has come to him. But if a parent or teacher has given him a wrong image his emotions are involved and he has trouble changing."[1]

Because spiritual training in early years is important, you must clarify your objectives and be sure these goals are reached through clear and careful teaching. To help set goals, you must understand the children, because you cannot teach them what they are not ready to receive. When a

---

1. Anna Mow, *Your Child from Birth to Rebirth*, p. 49.

child is ready to reach for a cup or a spoon, he is also ready to learn how to handle it. There is a readiness to learn to read, to write, and to play with others. If a child is pushed too soon, he becomes discouraged and frustrated as do his teachers and parents. Likewise, you must wait for children to exhibit their readiness for spiritual truth. You can help them be ready and receptive when you remember what young children are like. Review Chapter 3 to understand the child's physical, social, and mental development.

Look again at the nursery child

Remember that the nursery child believes most of what he hears. Through what he hears in Sunday school, his hunger for God can be encouraged and fed. He cannot understand symbolism, so teach him simply, using words that mean what he understands them to say. Preschool departments are not the places to talk about Jesus as the vine, the Captain, the Master, or the door. Let two- and three-year-olds know that Jesus is the Son of God and their best Friend.

Young children have a very short attention span. They will not listen to a Bible story for more than three to five minutes. They will learn through asking questions, so allow ample opportunity for pupils to talk at any time throughout your session.

Your example will mean more than almost anything else in the nursery department, because these children almost literally "catch" religion from you. How do you handle the Bible? How does your voice sound when you talk about the Lord or pray to Him? How do you show your love for the children?

Look again at children of four and five

A kindergartener's feelings are very near the surface, with fear as the most outstanding emotion. How much this child needs to know the Lord as his living, loving Friend and think about God in a very personal way. Four- and five-year-olds also believe what they hear. If Bible stories are chosen to meet their needs, they will believe and apply the spiritual truth being taught.

In working with preschoolers, move at their pace, planning well so that you do not abruptly ask them to interrupt their activities in order to meet your schedules. Preschoolers are unaware of time and need a quiet atmosphere to think well. They need praise, though not overdone, for right actions. No teacher should use fear as punishment, a rather common method with many parents who say, "The policeman (that lady, store clerk) will take you away if you don't behave." Certain Bible stories that are fearful must be left untold till the children are older.

Your own example will teach him quietly and consistently at every age. Be sure what your children observe backs up what you say!

The teacher of preschoolers is responsible for his own strong personal foundation in Bible truth, based on Scripture. No individual or single department can carry the total responsibility; every teacher must do his part to know the Word of God and learn how to share it with preschoolers. You must not let the pressure of time force you to concentrate so intently on what you want to accomplish that you lose sight of individual needs. The child will learn spiritual values at church, at home, and as he mingles with others who express their faith in a variety of ways.

You must recognize that you cannot regulate times for learning spiritual truths as you may some skills, such as learning to work a zipper, fasten a button, or tie a shoe. Attitudes and feelings can never be taught with this approach. That is why every children's worker needs to be aware of teachable moments, sensing the leading of the Holy Spirit. Singing a song, saying a verse, or praying is not worship unless the child's attitude is directed Godward.

How, then, can you teach spiritual truths and lead children to love God and worship Him? First, through your own example. Next, plan for the child to encounter and understand spiritual truth. Watch for reactions and relationships. Is there an unhappy or happy time when a child's thoughts can be directed to God? Any happy experience a preschooler has had may be an occasion to thank the Lord. A family or a personal problem expressed by a child may be a prayer request. Skill in guiding conversation is not learned overnight! To guide children to spiritual truth requires prayer, an openness and awareness of the Holy Spirit's leading, and experience with children. Many teachers who pray much about their teaching find themselves saying words and expressing ideas that have come to them only from the Holy Spirit. They admit that the ideas have not been part of their lesson preparation, but have been brought to mind as they talked with pupils and sensed their needs. The Holy Spirit is a wonderful Partner and Guide in our teaching!

Later chapters will deal with methods; this chapter will examine what a young child can learn. Cramming Bible facts into children's heads does not guarantee that Bible truths will be understood and assimilated. However, unless you have goals and objectives for a Bible-based learning program, you may accomplish very little in helping children. Goals make the difference! What can be accomplished in preschool years? The following goals have been compiled on the basis of age-group objectives as set up by both denominational and independent publishers of Sunday school literature.

What a child of two and three can learn

Even a young child is ready for many of the basic truths of Scripture if they are presented at his own level.

About God

He understands that God loves him.

He begins to show an attitude of trust in God and dependence on Him.

He understands that God is with him in all places.

He knows that God will hear when he talks to Him.

He recognizes that God made all things.

About Jesus Christ

He can understand that God sent Jesus.

He realizes that Jesus loves children and wants them to love Him.

He knows that Jesus can do hard things that no one else can do.

He grows in his realization that Jesus was a special baby.

He knows that Jesus can see him and hear him.

He understands that Jesus died, came back to life, and now lives in heaven.

On the basis of this knowledge, the child grows in love for the Lord Jesus and his desire to please Him.

About the Bible

He knows that the Bible is God's Book, a very special Book.

He wants to hear God's Word and do what God says in His Book.

He understands selected Bible stories and associates the Bible with feelings of love, reverence, and respect for God.

About his own attitudes and actions

He will pray simple, familiar prayers of petition and thanksgiving.

He can give his money to God's house.

He will grow in his desire to please God by obeying.

He is glad that Jesus loves him and is thankful for His daily care.

What a child of four and five can learn

Dr. Mary E. LeBar, author of Sunday school lessons for four- and five-year-olds, says that the only answer for the burdened Christian—young or old—is found in relying on the wonderful Saviour who answers every need of the human heart. We are never too young nor too old for His ministration. She stresses that at four and five, the need is not for heavy doctrine but for the comfort of His presence, His love and His care.

About God

This older preschooler builds on his growing knowledge of God to understand that God's love includes himself and also others.

He realizes that he can pray to God at any time and at any place.

He knows that God is the Creator and loving heavenly Father.

He begins to understand that God is the Sustainer of all things and provides him with the necessities of life. He is growing in his awareness that God cares for him through his parents and others.

He begins to feel a personal responsibility to God as the One he should love and want to obey. He is grateful to God for His provision and love.

The child of four or five is beginning to understand that God sent Jesus to die for everyone's sin, including his own.

He knows that sin is disobedience to God, and that God will forgive sin when he is genuinely sorry and asks for forgiveness.

About Jesus Christ

Adding to the spiritual foundation laid in earlier years, he knows that Jesus is God's Son and his best Friend who loves him. He realizes that Jesus is living now after dying for everyone's sin.

He understands that Jesus will help him obey (share, help).

The child knows that Jesus has the same power that God has.

He is learning to pray in the name of Jesus.

About the Bible

He knows that the Bible is a special Book and contains wonderful stories of Jesus.

He realizes that God's Word tells him what to do.

The kindergartener is growing in his ability to distinguish Bible stories as real, unlike other stories of imagination and fancy.

About his own attitudes or actions

The older preschooler is learning to pray at any time, in any place, and for everyone.

He can praise God by giving thanks.

He is growing in his concern for others, missions, church, and other children.

He is also growing in his love for God and Jesus, wanting to obey God, his parents, and teachers.

The child is also ready to show often that he can share, be kind, and tell others about Jesus.

He has a growing feeling of trust and security in God's love.

He wants to hear Bible stories, sometimes recalling favorites.

He can sometimes help explain how he should act on the basis of the spiritual truth taught in a story.

Belief and behavior

Children who love the Lord will change their behavior. A five-year-old was the despair of a local storekeeper. Every time this child came into his store, she played with displays until something was broken or the display toppled to the floor. Unfortunately, her parents did not see their responsibility in changing her conduct. However, one August day, the little girl came into the store, and the storekeeper, although not glad to see the child, realized he had not seen her for several months. She stayed with her mother and did more looking than touching. She responded to questions with polite answers. At last the storekeeper could stand it no longer. Rather bluntly he said, "Your daughter seems to have changed a lot this summer." Her mother, not a Christian, said, "Yes, we've noticed it too. I think it's because she went to vacation Bible school this summer."

After a child becomes a Christian—and some children do even as preschoolers—you may notice some behavioral changes, but you cannot expect perfection from these young children any more than you would from an adult. The preschooler will grow in his dependence on the Lord, in his frequent use of prayer, and in his desire to love the Lord and obey Him. The child is a new creature in Christ, but he is still a child. Teachers must be careful not to define as sin what is normal behavior for a preschooler. No teacher should ever try to control behavior by saying, "If you love Jesus, you will—" Assume that a child does love Jesus. Say, "Because we love Jesus, we want to take turns." Remember that Christian behavior is motivated by love for the Lord. Do not use a negative, corrective approach, implying that one who loves God will never have a wrong attitude or perform a wrong action.

Having learned what children can grasp in the categories of God, Jesus, the Bible, and attitudes, you must also realize that head knowledge is not enough. As you teach spiritual truth, you will want to watch for feelings or attitudes and actions. Some actions and attitudes are listed in the age-group objectives. Evaluate your teaching by the feelings and actions you are able to observe, realizing that many attitudes will be exhibited at home. Perhaps parents will share with you moments when their children expressed thankfulness to the Lord, love for Jesus, and a growing dependence on God. Parents may be the ones to notice the prayer life of their child, the Sunday school songs he sings, and the frequency with which he asks for a Bible story. A mother may be the one to report that her child asks every day, "Is today the day we go to church?" More than a few teachers have been overjoyed to find that Sunday school is a very important event in the lives of their preschoolers.

Your Sunday school curriculum will help you set weekly goals. You will not be teaching the whole Bible to preschoolers, nor will you be trying to develop a mature Christian in the few years a child spends in the preschool department. You will, however, be laying an enduring foundation and teaching through your own example. You are perhaps the most important aid in achieving spiritual objectives, because the children will learn more from your example and attitude than from anything else they experience in the preschool department.

How do you reach these goals and objectives? You do so week by week through finger plays, stories, music, prayer, moments of worship, creative activities, and visual aids—all presented after prayerful preparation. Every week, children should leave your department with new information but also with a clear understanding of a specific way in which they can demonstrate their love for and obedience to the Lord. Preschool teachers must have long-range goals, as exemplified in the age-group objectives, and also short-range goals, as identified in your weekly or unit teaching aims.

Teachers in the preschool departments need to understand the limitations of little children, even as they realize the importance of laying spiritual foundations. After he presents the story of Jesus and faithfully exhibits his own love for Him, a primary-department teacher may have the joy of seeing an actual decision for Christ. However, it is the training in these early years that has an important place in the child's finding the Lord as his Saviour and in his growing into the fullness of the Christian life.

A word about salvation

Every teacher who is a child of God longs for the day when his pupils come to know Christ as Saviour. However, you will need to pray and wait on the Holy Spirit lest you be tempted to deal with children in your own strength. "Though children are naturally more ready for salvation than adults, because of faith and dependence, rebirth is always supernatural. Preparation of heart, not a certain age, is the condition for salvation."[2] If you force a child to go through the outward motions of salvation, it is like prying open the bud of a flower before it is ready to bloom. As in human development, there is a prenatal period which precedes spiritual birth. You, a preschool teacher, have a great responsibility in this period.

The feelings of young children can be very easily stirred, and you can lead them through the outward form of accepting Christ without any spiritual rebirth taking place. After all, it requires a degree of maturity to understand sin, the meaning of the cross, and belief in the sacrificial death of Christ for the individual. In the fullness of God's time, a child will be brought to a conviction of sin, an understanding of what salvation is all about, and an opportunity to receive Christ as Saviour. Premature babies usually have a more difficult struggle for existence. Christian teachers do not want to put any obstacle in the way of their children to hinder them from having a valid conversion later on.

A poll of believers might indicate that some received Christ at the age of three or before. We must be careful not to judge the reality of an individual's testimony. However, statistics and experience indicate that most childhood conversions occur sometime between six and eleven. This does

2. Lois E. LeBar, *Children in the Bible School*, p. 176.

not mean that younger children cannot receive Christ but that it is not usual. Many four- and five-year-olds are just not ready to receive Jesus as Saviour, so you must be careful not to push them into meaningless decisions.

As young children grow in their understanding of the Bible and God's standard for Christians, they will realize that they cannot always please God. They will come to understand that they need help to keep from sinning. Their understanding and admitting the fact of sin and their own helplessness will lead the way to their acceptance of Christ as Saviour.

How will you deal with a young child who wants to receive Jesus as His Saviour? Talk to him alone. Explain that although God loves everyone, He cannot have sin (or badness) in heaven. But Jesus came and took the punishment for our badness. He died on the cross so that God can forgive our sin. When we tell Him we are sorry we have sinned, God forgives us and takes away our sin. How does the young child define his sin? This will be some indication to you of his understanding. Does he want to talk to God about it? If he does not, do not force him. The child is evidently feeling a need, but he may not be ready to receive Christ as Saviour. If the child does want to talk to God about his sin, encourage him to repeat a prayer after you, "Dear Lord, I know I have done wrong. I am sorry for my sin. I want You to be my Saviour and forgive me. In Jesus' name, Amen."

Be careful that you do not merely lead a child through the steps of receiving the Saviour. The working of the Holy Spirit is usually made evident by a concern on the child's part over his own sin and need. You cannot trifle with the Lord's working but must pray for His guidance. Preschoolers have not experienced much of life. As humans judge sin, they are not "big" sinners. You need not dwell on their sin as is done frequently with adults. Children may need only a simple explanation and suggestion—providing, of course, that the Holy Spirit is leading them.

There are many symbolic illustrations and stories available. Do not use them! Here is a good example of a story *not* to use. The story is told of a foolish frog who refused to dive to the bottom of the pond and hibernate for the winter. One morning, the pond's surface was frozen, and he could not dive. "Boys and girls, you don't want to be like that frog do you? One day it will be too late for you to ask Jesus to be your Saviour."

As a rule, the superintendent should choose a Sunday school curriculum that is Bible-based and evangelical. If the curriculum meets this standard, you can safely follow the lessons. Trained Christian educators have prayerfully written the lessons and usually have pre-tested them. These experienced teachers will help you to lead young children to grow spiritually, preparing them for the day when they will understand their need of a Saviour.

REACT

A compilation of letters written by children to God has furnished many adults with some good laughs. What would you do if you heard one of your preschoolers say, "God is an old man with many eyes"; or, "God lives at church and then goes back to heaven. That's all He sees"; or, "God is like a policeman. He don't want you to do nothing"?

ACT

1. Telling children about God is not enough. You must try to lead them to think about Him and trust Him. How can you relate your children's experiences to God? Think of one idea or experience a child has shared with you. Were you successful in directing the child's thoughts to God in this incident?
2. When you speak of the heavenly Father, young children draw some associations with their own earthly fathers. How well do you know the affection each child receives

or is denied by his parents? How should this influence your teaching? Are there reasons for not calling God the heavenly Father in some teaching situations?

5

Can Playing and Talking Be Teaching?

"Everything in its time" is a good slogan for preschool teachers. The time for play and guided conversation is in preschool years. The young child learns through play. He is discovering many things through the active use of his five senses. Why not use both play and conversation to help him understand and accept spiritual truth?

The next two chapters will deal with the more traditional teaching methods that most Sunday school teachers recognize. This chapter has been written to help you understand how very important educational play and guided conversation are in the learning experience of young children. Play is one way of learning that is more helpful to a child than any other. It is not only a way of learning, it is a way of life for the young child. Through play, the young child will learn in a short time what no one could teach him in many years.

Play as education

Because it is hard for adults to accept the concept of play as education, let's look at how adults play and how young children play. Recreation for adults is play because it is a change from their daily routines. Usually play costs the adult something in time, training, or performance: golf fees, tennis court rental, or pool admissions, are good examples. An adult plays to relax, to escape his workaday world.

What does an adult learn from play? Hopefully, he learns to be a better performer or at least to understand the rules of spectator sports such as hockey, football, or baseball. When an adult plays, enjoyment is given priority. If he works too hard at learning to play chess or to become proficient at scuba diving, he decides it is work and may withdraw from the activity. Most adults expect to exert less mental effort in recreation than they do on the job.

A child does not take this attitude. Play is his work! Through play, he learns more than he can in any other way. He learns how to balance on a bike. He learns how to deal with others at the housekeeping center. Painting teaches him about color, while sandbox and water play introduce him to texture, structure, measurement, and perhaps new words. Through play, the young child gains information, finds emotional expression, understands social situations, and is freed for motor activity—his muscles move.

Your concern as a teacher is with the content of play and how to use play as a teaching method. Christian education is not primarily concerned with "free play." This is play of a child's own choosing and, while helpful to the child, may not move him in the direction of the goals and objectives described in chapter 4. Christian education is concerned with educational or structured play—play with a purpose. Of course, we include some free play in our programs, but we are dealing with important spiritual truths, and so we plan play with a purpose.

Play as an educational device has historical support. From Froebel to Piaget, play is recognized as a means of helping a child mature. Dr. Bernard Spodek, Professor of Early Childhood Education, University of Illinois, says,

> Traditionally, the field of early childhood education has been characterized by its support of play as an educational tool. Teachers at the nursery and kindergarten level organize their classrooms for play activities in the belief that through these activities young children can best learn what they are expected to learn. Even in the primary grades where direct verbal instruction is a more acceptable mode of instruction, play is still considered to be an important educative device and many of the instruction activities are developed in the form of learning games.[1]

Remember that for a play situation to be educationally useful, you must guide and supervise. It is not enough for a Christian teacher to agree that play is a good means of teaching and learning; you must also know what type of play helps learning. Unless you can begin to think of play as a learning technique, we may always feel guilty because, in our thinking, we are letting the children play when they should be seated in chairs, learning by rote. (If play to you is only recreation, you will want to read this chapter more than once.) Let's remember, play to the child is work. He throws

1. Bernard Spodek, *Teaching in the Early Years* (Englewood Cliffs, N.J.: Prentice-Hall, 1972) p. 199.

himself into play as desperately as does a runner in a race, a scientist at a microscope, or a machinist at a lathe. Play is the young child's business, and he works at his play more hours than most breadwinners! The play pattern of young children is not stupid, silly, or a waste of time. God has planned for children to grow through playing. When a young child learns to climb a slide, put a puzzle together, or catch a ball, he is learning through play.

Jesus Christ recognized play as part of childhood, for He planned child development. He knew that when children played parts in the adult world, they were also getting acquainted with life. He recognized children's desire to take adult roles when, in reference to their pretend games, He said, "They are like unto children sitting in the marketplace, and calling one to another, and saying, 'We have piped unto you, and ye have not danced; we have mourned to you, and ye have not wept'" (Lk 7:32). When the Lord identified the glory of the future He said, "And the streets of the city shall be full of boys and girls playing in the streets thereof" (Zec 8:5).

Through play, a child gains new experiences, discovers new possibilities in the use of materials, develops his personality, and thinks constructively. A child learns to know his own body—how to master it and use it. He discovers that his arms can throw, his hands can hold, and his feet can walk. Whenever a child plays the role of another, he is feeling that person's situation. Sunday school lesson writers often suggest that young children play out situations to get the feeling of reality, the "you are there" quality. Why else would a teacher lead children to "march through the wilderness" or play the crowning of King Joash?

When children use blocks to build the wall of Jericho, they remember the story and learn more of what a walled city may have been. This "play" experience will help children more than any number of words describing the city. When children pretend to carry a basket-boat to a river and wait in the rushes for the princess, they have a sense of realism about the story of Moses. If children pretend to be tiny seeds huddled on the ground, awaiting God's sun and rain, they have deeper appreciation for God's plan for growing things. When a four- or five-year-old draws a picture of himself helping a parent, he has a better understanding of what it means to help than if he merely hears a teacher say, "We want to help at home, don't we?"

Notice, too, that children change in their play as they mature. Is a four-year-old interested in playing peek-a-boo? Why not? What are some of the toys that children leave behind as they develop? Two- and three-year-olds discard rattles, teething rings, washable books, and playpens as they are ready for wheeled toys, blocks, simple puzzles, and art materials. Play is progressive, a learning process that utilizes all their senses.

Young children are special. They don't fit into groups who will study workbooks or listen to many words. As stated in *Creative Bible Teaching,* "They're short on words and need to learn ideas in association with activities that will give the ideas meaning."[2]

In Sunday school, plan a variety of activities for preschoolers, all of which work toward the aim or goal of the morning. Many of these activities will look like play, but they should be carefully planned learning experiences that use eyes, ears, and many muscles in growing bodies. When two- and three-year-olds gravitate to interest centers, they should find materials that teach. Books at the book center should be chosen carefully to include some of the background needed for the Bible story. Toys and objects at each center will help accent the daily aim, and there will be teachers present to guide conversation so that it is meaningful.

You as a lone teacher do not need to struggle with the

2. Lawrence O. Richards, *Creative Bible Teaching* (Chicago: Moody, 1971), p. 158.

problem of planned or educational play. You do not need to determine materials nor plan all of the guided conversation, because a good Sunday school curriculum for preschoolers should provide you with an abundance of suggestions. Sunday school should be fun for preschoolers, but the fun has a purpose. It is not planned merely to entertain or "keep the children quiet." If an activity does not tie into the lesson aim, it should be reevaluated and probably discarded. Finger plays, records, art activities, playing out stories, and even helping to return materials to storage may all appear as play to the child, but you, the teacher, know better. And planning carefully for these activities is not play for you!

You will notice that prayer, singing, and other forms of worship are not included in the play category. If a child plays at worshiping the Lord, you deprive him of the reality which must accompany his relationship to God. Is the distinction clear? Play is a means of teaching and learning, but *it is not* a way of being. There must be adequate provision in the preschool schedule for moments of deep and meaningful communication with the Lord and true worship and praise to God.

Guided conversation

Guided conversation is the second important teaching method sometimes overlooked. What is guided conversation? I use the term to mean conversation that is guided to a spiritual emphasis. It is easy to talk with a young child about his puppy, a trip to the zoo, going fishing with Daddy, or wearing new shoes. However, many conversations with young children can be guided to help a child think of God. This is not easy! It requires a close relationship with the Lord, an understanding of children, and an awareness of the Bible content you are teaching. Let's illustrate.

Charles had a difficult situation in kindergarten. Most of the children had trouble with Lester, an aggressive five-year-old who bullied the children, but the teacher did not seem to realize it. He was the pusher on the playground, the puncher in little unobserved ways, the tease, and the snatcher of the kindergarten room. One Sunday, Charles related this incident about Lester to his teacher.

"Lester's a mean boy at our school. But know what I did? I told him his picture was the prettiest of all."

"Why, Charles," said the teacher, "you were remembering, 'Be ye kind' weren't you? Jesus wants us to be kind to others."

"Yep," said Charles, very satisfied with himself, "and Lester didn't push me that day."

This incident illustrates the guided conversation used by the teacher and also demonstrates how five-year-old Charles was adjusting to a social situation. Only as you are in close contact with the Lord, pray about your children, and really live at the child's level will you be able to use guided conversation effectively. Notice that most Sunday school lesson writers recognize this technique and include illustrations in their lessons.

Guided conversation requires a listening ear to discover where the child is in his experience and thoughts. You also need a listening heart to be ready for God to help you know what to say. "Spiritual conversation" does not consist in reviewing a Bible story or speaking in Bible verses, but it does mean being aware of God's working in your own life. If your thoughts are directed toward Him, you will find it easy to speak of Him.

Handling types of behavior

Teaching would be much easier if the pupils sat quietly, drank in what you said, and participated only when asked. Perhaps this happens in adult classes, but it never happens in the preschool departments. Because preschoolers are engaged in activity and because there are many social amenities these little people have not learned, there may be conflicts.

Remember that two- and three-year-olds do not like to play in groups. Several children may join in an activity, but most nursery children will prefer parallel play. In parallel play the children play near each other, seeming to enjoy the presence of other children. However, each child is interested in his own activity, which may be the same as the child's next to him or may be a different activity. Two children may work puzzles without any interest in one another, or they may build with blocks or push wheeled toys. Two- and three-year-olds seem to become aware of one another only when the presence of another child is important. Bouncing on a teeter-totter is one example. Four- and five-year-olds are aware of one another and generally enjoy playing together, although it may be with only one other child. Then, too, some children seem to enjoy being onlookers, watching the other children at play but playing little themselves. The onlookers and the solitary players will become involved in their own good time. Do not force them, but do invite them to participate at least one or more times during every lesson.

The young child is developing his concepts of "me," "you," and "us." A ten-year-old can look at a picture of Jesus and say, "Jesus wants all the children to love Him." However, a two may grab the picture, hold it possessively while saying, "My Jesus!" The same "my" attitude will carry over into learning activities and use of materials. You cannot force a child to share! Taking a toy from one child and giving it to another while the first child howls is not sharing. It is merely proving that you are stronger.

How can you lead children to share? Often with nursery children, you need to provide more than one of an object. A young child does not understand that his turn will come. He panics when he does not have what he wants. He will outgrow this attitude as he matures. Do not feel that you must teach children to share. When a child grabs a toy and refuses to give it up, you may say, "Mike, Tommy would like to play with the red truck too. When you are through, will you let him have it?" Mike may agree that he will, but you had best provide a blue truck for Tommy to use while he waits. Then when Mike sees that you treat all children fairly and that he can have the truck without fear of losing it, he will slowly but surely learn to share. This will take weeks, perhaps months.

Some children will be aggressive, lashing out at others. Why? As you figure out the "why," remove the child from the situation if it allows him to hurt other children. You may be able to hold the preschooler or take him by the hand to another area of the room. It is these unexpected situations that make it imperative to have enough teachers. A child becomes aggressive under a variety of circumstances: when he fears a new situation, when he is being asked to do more than he can really do, when something frustrates him, when another child does not accept him, and when he cannot have his own way. Keep calm with the aggressive child. You may abhor his biting habit, but you must continue to love him. If you have separated him from the other children, you may say, "Dan, we don't let children bite. You cannot bite other children, and I will not let anyone bite you. As long as you feel like biting, you had better stay here and look at this book [or some other quiet activity]." Isolate the child, but let him feel your love. There is little value in forcing a child to say "I'm sorry" when he really is not. Try to help the child save face and rejoin the group.

An aggressive child is certain to attract your attention, but the timid child may not. However, you have a responsibility to a timid child. He, too, has come to learn. As a conscientious teacher, you are committed to do your best for every child—not merely the bothersome one or the one who is easy to love.

The timid child stands by when he may want to be involved. A timid girl may give up a doll she wants to an aggressive toy-grabber. The timid child is fearful of new experiences or difficult tasks, and so he withdraws. Perhaps a timid child comes from a home where adults are constantly cautioning, "Don't touch!" "Don't get dirty!" "Be careful!" Naturally that child is conditioned to be an onlooker in your Sunday school room. What can you do about it? Give the child the security of your calm, loving attitude toward him. See that your Sunday school program has enough routine so that he will feel comfortable. If the child's timidity is related to his lack of knowledge about how to do something or how to use equipment, do not mention his ignorance. Instead, quietly explain or demonstrate, keeping your comments impersonal. To say, "You're a big boy. You can do it," may only intensify his feeling about his own inadequacy. Be nearby to help the timid child, but do not flutter over him or let him constantly depend on you.

What if a child has a tantrum in Sunday school? Four- and five-year-olds have usually learned enough self-control to avoid tantrums. However, some two- and three-year-olds lose their self-control and kick, cry, and toss about. Recognize that the child may be very tired or perhaps has run into a frustration he cannot handle. Usually tantrums are caused because a child cannot do what he wants. The tantrum may be triggered by not being given a toy or failing to accomplish what he was sure he could do. A three-year-old whose shoelace broke was inconsolable and indulged in a tantrum. Sometimes handwork that is too complicated causes children to lose control.

What can you do? It is up to the parents to decide whether isolation or spanking is the remedy at home. At Sunday school, you will want to stay with the child, waiting quietly for him to gain self-control. Neither bribing nor condemning him has a place in your treatment. If necessary, remove the child from the room, but stay with him. Let him know that he can return to the group when he feels better. You may find it helpful to offer him a drink or a book to look at. If a child consistently throws tantrums, you will want to observe the home and perhaps ask for help.

Above all, remember that each child is precious to the Lord. Most of the children will return your love for them. And all of them will be easier to work with as they mature and as you gain experience.

REACT

1. What is your assessment of play? Do you regard it as something to amuse the children?
2. What experience have you had in guided conversation?

ACT

1. Continue to work on the art of guided conversation. Perhaps you are already using it more than you realize. Remember, you will not preach, but speak as naturally as you would to a friend your own age.
2. Have your children been learning through play? List some of the ways you have used it. Now read the next chapters to see how you can teach through play.

6

How Will You Teach?

Is your teaching stuffed with facts, or is it full of ideas? Are you interested in pouring what you know into young minds and having it set like concrete, or are you concerned with helping children think and discover? One secret of good teaching is to know the pupil and respect him.

Teaching preschoolers takes time! Yes, the Bible stories are simple, and you certainly know more than your pupils, but what about the materials and preparation? You must be prepared *before* the first child arrives. If you work with older children, you can ask them to arrange chairs, distribute books, or give them another task while you write on the chalkboard or find a filmstrip projector. You cannot follow this procedure with preschoolers. They demand all of your attention. Every visual aid, every interest center, every part of the Sunday school hour must be ready *before* they arrive.

Your preschoolers come on Sunday morning ready to learn through their senses—seeing, hearing, touching, and sometimes smelling or tasting. Your materials should help them learn in these ways. This means more preparation! Preschoolers love to learn and will do so with enthusiasm, because they have a sense of wonder and a drive to explore that has not been dulled. Young children, unlike their older brothers and sisters, are not concerned with succeeding in a competitive sense. Because preschoolers recognize that they are learners, they are not frustrated by their own ignorance. They may be frustrated by not being able to do a task, such as cutting or folding, but they are not frustrated because they do not know certain facts or recall specific information. This chapter will explain some typical Sunday school programs for preschoolers and describe activities which are usually conducted in a group. Chapter 7 will detail learning through interest-center or learning-center activities and expressional activities.

The successful Sunday school program for preschoolers must include *presession*—some activity when the first child arrives. Most important is the *Bible story*—the purpose for Sunday school, Bible knowledge and spiritual growth. *Worship,* an emotional response to the Lord, may occur at any time during the session. Then *expression* takes place to give a child an opportunity to express what he has learned. Depending on the age of the children, the curriculum, space available, and the number of children and teachers, the time for each part will vary. However, every child should receive *instruction,* enjoy *fellowship,* have an opportunity to *worship,* and be encouraged to *express* what he has learned. Expression is not merely reciting facts, but lets the child show what the lesson means to him. Sometimes expressional activities are called Bible learning activities.

What makes up a good session for preschoolers? You will have music, prayer, Bible story, moments of worship, individual activities, playing the story, interest centers, and various other learning activities. The parts of the hour should be put together for the pupils' interests not for the teachers' convenience. In planning the parts of the hour, be sure to include active as well as quiet times.

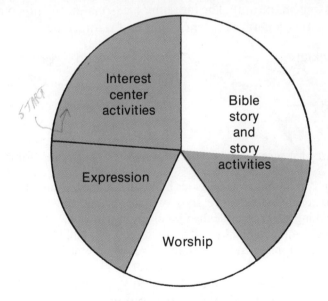

Fig. 1. How the class session is divided.

Active times, when the pupil is doing, are shaded.
Quiet times, when the pupil spends more time listening, are unshaded.

A good curriculum for preschoolers will have activities that the particular age—two, three, four, or five—can understand and perform. For example, it would be ridiculous to expect two-year-olds to skip to music or to work together in writing a song. Five-year-olds will be able to skip and to help write music, but they would be bored with the picture books and the simple stories two-year-olds can understand. Curriculum writers have studied children and know the materials and methods best suited to each age.

A good curriculum is planned to make every moment count. One main aim for each lesson is another good criterion for a curriculum. The aims for individual lessons should, of course, help develop the unit aim. Notice in your curriculum material how the unit aim is an "umbrella" for all of the lessons in the unit. The individual lessons should present parts of the general aim, enriching and reinforcing it.

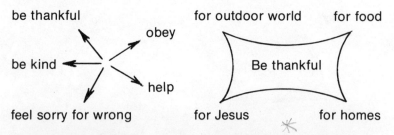

Fig. 2. How individual lessons build toward the unit aim. If you teach individual lessons, without a unit aim, your teaching may resemble the first diagram. However, if you have a unit aim and keep it in mind, you will build on the aim, reinforcing and reviewing it through several lessons.

The aims for a unit should not only include knowledge goals—what a child should know—but must also recognize that a child needs to respond through his feelings. It is not enough to tell young children the story of Jesus stilling the storm, you also want them to feel more love for and confidence in the Lord Jesus.

Another key to a good morning's session is flexibility. If the moment seems to demand music, a finger play, or a relaxing activity, the prepared teacher is ready. Sessions for two- and three-year-olds cannot be run on a rigid schedule. There will be Sundays when four- and five-year-olds do not respond in the way you planned for them to react. Be flexible! Remember you are teaching children, not lessons. If you are constantly urging the children on to another activity because you have planned a full morning, you are really building up tension. These little people have no sense of time; that is why so many preschoolers dawdle.

It is impossible, in a book dealing with children from two through five, to describe a specific program for you to use. Here is what a typical program for three-year-olds may look like:

Individual or small group activities—10 minutes
Together time—25 minutes
Expressional time—20 minutes
Closing time—5 minutes

A program for two-year-olds may look like this, because they need many more individual and small group activities:

Individual activities—40 minutes
Group activities—10 minutes

We must recognize that not all two- and three-year-olds will join in group activities. Do not insist that they do, but frequently invite them to join and be sure that the group activities are so attractive that children will want to participate.

In the department for four- and five-year-olds, a typical program may look like this:

Individual and small group activities—10 minutes
Group activities—25 to 30 minutes
Small group activities—10 to 15 minutes

Another publisher, however, may present a program for four- and five-year-olds that looks like this:

Bible learning activity time—20 minutes
Together time—20 minutes
Bible story activity time—20 minutes

Follow the schedule suggested in your curriculum. You may want to make changes, but first understand what the curriculum writer is trying to accomplish. Be sure the children have plenty of opportunity to participate, because preschoolers cannot sit quietly to hear an adult talk, talk, *talk!* If you pride yourself on having a "quiet" group of four- and five-year-olds who sit around a table listening to your story and then quietly color some handwork, you are guilty of stifling the children and omitting some of the best learning techniques available. "Quiet children" is not the mark of the most effective learning. Perhaps the difference lies in the teacher's viewpoint. Are you proud of what *you* have *taught,* or are you happy for what the *children* have *learned?*

(Many churches are providing a second hour for preschoolers. Some keep the same time schedule followed in Sunday school, but vary the activities. Some teachers use the second hour to review and reinforce Sunday school lessons, incorporating additional art activities. There are also publishers who offer a carefully planned second hour program to correlate with the Sunday school material.)

What is the scene in your room when the first child appears? How do you greet the children and help them enter into the day's activities? In some preschool departments, a child gives his offering when he enters. Preschoolers usually arrive individually, not in a group, and are ready for individual activities. These individual or small group activities are described in chapter 7. Remember that the individual activity time or interest-center learning takes place at the beginning of the hour. For two-year-olds, it may be the greater part of the hour. The two teaching-learning methods discussed in chapter 5, play and guided conversation, will probably be used throughout the Sunday school hour, but they are always used in the individual or small group activities. Check the schedule on page 71 which most resembles your organization of the Sunday school hour.

Now let's turn our attention to the specific activities and teaching of the large group time. Some curriculums call the large group time "together time," "worship activities," or "sharing time." Regardless of the title, teachers plan this part of the session. The large group time will include the Bible story, music Bible verse, perhaps applicational or conduct story, prayer, playing out the story or role playing, often special moments of fellowship to recognize visitors or celebrate a birthday.

The younger the child, the smaller the group. Two- and three-year-olds will do best when they are with no more than ten other children. These young children may seem to enjoy an exciting, stimulating hour, but afterward, they may be exhausted.

What about music?

You will use music in both the large group and the small group or individual activities. However, the same criteria apply wherever music is used. Music must be more than rhythm; the words must mean something to the young child. One song that meets the standard for music and words is "The Wonder Song."

> Oh, who can make a flower?
> I'm sure I can't, can you?
> Oh, who can make a flower?
> No one but God 'tis true!

A group of children will enjoy singing this song, but you may also use it with one child at the nature center. The song can be used for a variety of nature objects if you change the word *flower* to *stone, shell, star,* or other object.

All preschoolers enjoy music, but four- and five-year-olds are most likely to join you in singing. Two- and three-year-olds will listen to you, but few of them will sing with you. Listening to music is an experience all young children enjoy. The ways of listening and the necessary equipment will be discussed in chapter 7.

What is good music for preschoolers? First, the words must say something to them. This means that the words will be within the vocabulary of the children, and the ideas in any song will be simple and few. Examine some hymns, and you will discover that there may be as many as eight ideas in one stanza. Preschoolers need one simple thought.

> Christmas bells are ringing,
> Happy children singing,
> Jesus came from heaven,
> Jesus came from heaven.
> Jesus came from heaven.
> Christmas bells are ringing,
> Happy children singing,
> Jesus, Baby Jesus, was born
> On Christmas Day.[1]

Why is the above song better for four- and five-year-olds than for two- and three-year-olds?

> A helper, a helper
> Jesus wants me for a helper.
> A helper, a helper,
> I'll be a helper for Him.

What makes this a good song for two- and three-year olds? The music and rhythm of both songs are also good for preschoolers.

Children need to learn new songs to accept the new and expanding ideas being taught. They need to sing songs to learn spiritual truths and to make these truths part of their thinking and feeling. How can this be done?

If your children sing one song after another, or hear you

---

1. "Jesus Came From Heaven," © 1957, world rights reserved, Scripture Press Foundation. Used by permission.

sing them, without any reason to sing, you have a song time, but it is not a learning or thinking time. If your children sing in this way, they may never really concentrate on the meaning of the words or sing with understanding. Before teaching a song to children in a group situation, the children should have heard the song several times. How? The pianist may use the song as quiet music; perhaps you could sing the song at a strategic moment, or you may use the words of the song in guided conversation. Not until a child has really heard the message of a song can he begin to learn the song for himself. This is especially important for three-, four-, and five-year-olds. If the children hear the song several times as adults sing it, they will learn it naturally and correctly.

How many songs should you use? Another criterion for a good curriculum is the number of meaningful songs that are introduced to help children discover and review Bible truth. If you can make up simple tunes for the Bible memory verses, the verses will become more meaningful to your children. You will not want to use more songs than your children can enjoy, but you must not repeat favorite songs endlessly. Remember, a song is a good way to introduce a new concept.

A word of caution about symbolism belongs in a discussion of music for young children. The preschoolers, two through five, are thinking concretely and literally. Songs such as "I Am the Door," "Fishers of Men," "Give Me Oil in My Lamp," "This Little Light of Mine," and others similar should be ruled out on the basis of using words that are figurative. What child wants oil from a can or bottle squirted over the lamp in the family room? How can Jesus be a door? Wait until children are nine or older before introducing songs with symbolic language.

How will you use prayer?

Prayer is important at any time! The brief sentence prayer at the interest center is just as important and sometimes more meaningful to the individual child than prayer in the large group. Even two- and three-year-olds may offer to pray. Their prayers may be incoherent or far removed from the topic at hand, but if the prayer is their sincere expression, be sure to welcome their voluntary contributions.

Preschoolers pray very realistically. Accept their prayers without suggesting other words or other "improvements." "Help Mommy cook good." "Help Daddy fix my doll." "Be with my daddy on the plane." Feeling must precede praying. You cannot expect a child who feels nothing for God to be willing to talk to Him. But you can expect a child who feels strongly for someone or about something to want to pray about it.

When you lead in prayer, your prayers must be short and meaningful. Give one idea at a time, in one sentence at a time! And limit your ideas! Sometimes you will want to use a prayer poem. At another time you may want to use a Bible verse to introduce prayer. You may say, "We love You, Jesus, because You first loved us. Thank You for—"

While folded hands, closed eyes, and bowed heads help children to concentrate attention on the prayer and its purpose, you need not insist on this posture in small group or individual activities. Help your children to realize that they can pray standing, kneeling, walking, sitting, lying down, or in any posture at any place or time.

Preschoolers can be helped to a balanced prayer life. They can be taught to *thank* God. Two- and three-year-olds may ask God for things (*petition*) or they may continually pray, "God bless—" However, four- and five-year-olds can learn about *confession* for wrongdoing—being sorry for sin. Some kindergarteners may be able to pray simple prayers of *adoration*. Many preschoolers will *intercede* for others as they pray for the needs of missionaries, families, and friends.

Help children grow in their prayer life by using these forms of prayer: petition, thanksgiving, intercession, adoration, and confession. Part of your job is to enlarge a child's prayer life. One teacher did it this way. Five-year-old Brent continually prayed only for himself and his family. One day the teacher said to him, "Brent, do you know anyone else who needs God's help?" Brent did. He only needed the suggestions from his teacher to become a real intercessor for others.

What about Bible verses for preschoolers?

Do you want a child merely to say a verse or to know what that verse means for him? Your answer to this question helps you select Bible verses. Children can be taught long involved verses. They can learn by rote, but if Bible memory verses are to speak to the child, they must say something that he can live by. Check the verses in your curriculum. Remember God has said, "Be ye doers of the Word" (Ja 1:22). Is it true that hearing or memorizing without doing should be avoided? The Bible verses in your curriculum should be used frequently in guided conversation, as an introduction to prayer or to a song, and certainly whenever possible in the Bible story.

Why tell stories?

Just telling a story will not be enough. You should tell stories to teach. The Lord Jesus told many stories to help His listeners learn. The lost coin, the lost sheep, and the lost son in Luke 15 are examples of His stories. We tell stories because young children cannot absorb Bible truth unless it is in a meaningful setting. Stories provide the setting and the action that preschoolers need. The children's experiences are too limited and their way of thinking too literal to allow them to understand some of the deep truths of Scripture. Paul wrote, "All scripture is given by inspiration of God, and is profitable for doctrine, for reproof, for correction, for instruction in righteousness" (2 Ti 3:16). No little child can grasp what Paul wrote to Timothy, but the child can understand the reality of the Bible through the story of Josiah hearing the Scripture read and his response to it. Josiah's is only one of several Bible stories related to love for God's Word.

Bible stories present the information we want children to have about the Lord and what He wants them to be. Stories are one of the most effective teaching methods for preschoolers. The stories we tell must be true to the Bible, because the Word of God is the only authentic source of God's direction to us. The story must be told accurately, because we do not want children to have "facts" which they must unlearn at a future time.

Curriculum writers choose stories that teach Bible truth and are understandable to young children. A story for two-year-olds will be little more than twenty-five to thirty sentences—all short. Four- and five-year-olds will have much longer stories. Sometimes a Bible story in the curriculum will omit some facts, or the writer may have added information that is not in the Bible passage. Is this wrong? It is if the facts omitted or the information added really change the story. However, there are times when additional ideas make the story more understandable and really are things that could have happened. The Bible does not expressly state that the nets used by Jesus' fishermen friends went *swish, swish,* yet you would be justified in adding such a detail to the story. Adults bring a background of experience and information to the Bible facts. However, a young child does not have this experience that fills in the setting, feelings, sights, and sounds. To make the story real to inexperienced children, it is justifiable to suggest some setting, as long as that setting is compatible with the known Bible facts. Nets do make a swishing sound, donkeys do walk with a clopping sound, and children in Bible days ran and shouted even as children do today. However, additions to a Bible story, whether added by the teller or writer, must always conform to true biblical customs, history, and geography.

The added facts must be probable in the circumstances of the narrative.

Sometimes a writer omits details that would detract from the main teaching of the story or that would cause undue emotional response from little children. For example, there are several stories that could be told in a way to emphasize fear: the robbers on the Jericho road, the thundering hordes of Egyptians who drowned, even Jacob's lonely trip can be told as a fearsome experience. Because little children easily become emotionally involved, curriculum writers have told the stories in language children can understand and have included only the events that help accomplish the lesson aim.

Curriculum writers also suggest ways of preparing children for the unfamiliar. If a lamp, Oriental house, net, shepherd, or other biblical object or custom is vital to the story, the writer will show you how to acquaint the children with this information in an interest center or through an individual activity. (Individual learning activities will be discussed in the next chapter.) Never assume that young children know more than they really do. Test if you are in doubt. Let a child tell you what a well looks like, how a sling was used, and where people slept.

Preschoolers are interested in the action of the story. They are not too concerned with the where and when. Skip difficult names, talking about Moses' mother, Hannah's husband, and the wicked king (Jehoiakim), for example. Emphasize the action words and conversation, omitting long descriptions. Avoid asking rhetorical questions in the story, because they will interrupt the flow of events and invite the children to interrupt. If you do use questions, the children will answer, and you may have difficulty getting back to the story. Do not correct yourself if some detail slips your mind. If it is important, look for an opportunity to weave it into the story later.

Do hold your Bible or have it near at hand when you tell a

story. Sometimes show older preschoolers where the story appears in the Bible. Never read the Bible story from your teaching manual! Notice how a good curriculum applies the story without moralizing but by coming to a conclusion that helps a child grasp the reality of the biblical event.

Teachers have more trouble in starting stories than they do with any other part of the story. Never start by saying, "Once upon a time," or, "Long, long ago." These phrases make the story seem unreal. A good curriculum will show you how to begin a story, giving the children a reason for listening. This approach does not give away the story. An approach that tells more than it should might be, "Today we'll hear about a baby who was hidden in a basket so that a wicked king could not find him." Take a second look. How many ideas appear in that one sentence? Too many for preschoolers. Here is an approach that suggests a reason for listening, "Let's find out how a big sister took care of her baby brother."

After the story, you will want to use an appropriate follow-up activity. One of the best ways to help children feel the story is to play it. Your children will find it easy to imagine the setting. Four- and five-year-olds will have no difficulty with this type of story play, and three-year-olds will enjoy doing what they can. After the baby Moses story, let the children pretend to be Miriam. They may enjoy being the mother and placing a pretend baby and his bed in a pretend river. It will not bother preschoolers for everyone to take the part of the main character. However, if the children suggest taking turns at playing the main character, recognize their request and play the story this way. Your children will not want to play all of the events of the stories—just the action parts and the climax. Of course you will never ask a child to play the part of the Lord Jesus. No human can take His place. Ask another teacher to read or repeat the words Jesus said. For example, all of the children will enjoy lying on the floor or drooping in their chairs as you tell of the nobleman's sick son. Then when the teacher says, "Jesus made the little boy well," your children will love jumping to their feet, feeling well and strong again.

Sometimes a finger play will help the children review the story and be a part of it. Always overlearn a finger play so that you can give it as a spontaneous, joyous experience. Do not expect preschoolers to learn the words of a finger play. You say it, and demonstrate the motions. Your children will enjoy watching, some will repeat it with you, and most of them will do the motions.

After hearing and playing the story, your children are ready for the type of activities suggested in the next chapter.

REACT

1. Did you miss a section on worship? Why do you think it was omitted?
2. If children are to love the Bible, they must be led to think of it as a special Book that tells about God and Jesus. Do the activities described in this chapter help a child feel that way about the Bible?
3. Does it bother you to tell the same stories more than once? Though adults may tire of a particular story, young children do not. Even the Christmas story is really a new story to many little children.

ACT

1. How many times can worship take place during a Sunday school hour? We define worship as a time when a child is aware of God, who He is, and is responding to Him with love. Does worship take place in your Sunday school? When? Observe to see if worship is a frequent experience. It should be.
2. How do you help your children remember the story and "feel" it? How often do you

use a finger play or story play, playing out the story, to accomplish this purpose? If you have not tried it, will you?

7

What Are Individual or Small Group Activities?

The Lord Jesus taught the *multitudes* (Mk 6:34). He taught the *small group* of twelve (Mk 3:13-14). He also taught the *individual* —Peter, in this instance—(Mt 18:21).

Typical Sunday school programs for preschoolers include activities for large and small groups. The Bible story, music, and worship activities are usually planned for all of the children, a large group. Then interest center or learning activities are conducted for small groups. (The term *learning center* as used here is not synonymous with the learning centers used in public schools, where an abundance of material is available for individual study. However, *interest center* does not always convey the idea that a learning experience should take place.) Check chapter 6 to identify typical Sunday school programs and select the one most like your Sunday school session. The younger the child, the more time he will spend in small group or individual activities.

Many of the small group activities seem to be play, but remember that playing is learning (see chap. 5). The preschool teacher makes the best use of guided conversation in the small group or with an individual child. Notice how Terry's teacher used guided conversation to help Terry recognize God's care: Terry hurried to the art table as soon as he entered the Sunday school room. "What would you like to use?" asked the teacher at this center. Without comment, three-year-old Terry took a green crayon and a large sheet of paper. Quickly he drew green grass across the bottom of the sheet. Then he selected a brown crayon and covered the paper with slashing rain. The teacher said, "Terry, tell me about your picture." As Terry described his "splashy" walk to Sunday school, the teacher made meaningful comments about God's gift of rain and our need of it.

Remember that guided conversation requires a listening ear to discover where the child is in his experience and thoughts. A teacher who uses guided conversation to an advantage must be a child of God who is walking in close communion with Him. If your thoughts are directed toward Him, you should find it easy to speak of Him in terms the child understands.

If possible, plan enough interest or learning centers to give the children a choice of activities. There must be a teacher at every center! Preschoolers need an adult to encourage, to converse with the children, and to see that all have an opportunity to use the materials. You may have any or all of the following centers, depending on your space and personnel: art, book, puzzle, block, housekeeping, music, and nature. It would be unusual to have all of these centers on any given Sunday, but you may have as many as four or five. You will not want to set up centers or plan activities without asking yourself, "What is the purpose of this center or activity?" You must also decide what value the children will get from it and whether it is suited to the age group. Cutting and pasting, for example, is an activity better for five-year-olds than for two-year-olds. Be sure to evaluate the activities by asking, "What do I want the children to learn, to feel, or to experience in this activity? Is it correlated with the aim for the day?" You will also watch to see how your children respond to the various centers and activities.

Watch as the preschoolers enter their room. Most of them will be accompanied by parents and will be coming into the room one at a time. Many preschoolers give their offering as soon as they come into the room and before joining an activity. (The offering may be dedicated during a worship time.) Having preschoolers give their offering first is a good time-saving practice, eliminating the problem of lost coins. However, you must make the act of giving meaningful. Children do not understand if they merely deposit their coins in a box which is later emptied by a big man who comes to the door of the room. How can this money be their gift to Jesus?

Choose a container that has some relationship to the purpose of the offering. It may be a church bank or a receptacle made from a missionary curio. By all means provide a closed container so that children are not tempted to play with the coins. If you display a picture near the container it will help the children remember the reason for the offering. You do not want any child to think that he is paying his way into Sunday school. The picture may show the pastor, your church, people going into the church, a missionary supported by your church, or some object for which the money is used. A teacher should talk with the child as he deposits his money. After giving his offering, a child is ready to choose a learning center. All centers should be easily accessible to the children.

The nature center

Arrange your nature center on a low table or shelf. You may include an aquarium with fish; one or more flowers or leaves; a bird's nest, a magnifying glass and small objects; a prism to reflect the sunlight; a cocoon; a terrarium; and/or a variety of seeds. (Supervise two-year-olds carefully, or they may try eating some of the smaller objects.) Vary the items, choosing those that will relate to your lesson.

The housekeeping center

The housekeeping center should include child-size furniture that enables preschoolers to play out what they know best in life—their own homes. Dolls, chairs, a doll bed, a stove, a cabinet-sink or stove-sink combination, and plastic dishes are good basic materials. Some teachers add dress-up clothes, play dough, and other materials, but no material should be provided unless it has value for the children.

As a child pretends, he reveals some understanding of how he feels in certain situations. When you suggest activities to play out at this center, you are helping the child identify with some experiences that correlate with the lesson. You may suggest that the children put the dolls (and household) to bed as an activity that correlates with the Bible story of Jacob's lonely trip. If the children prepare a pretend meal and serve it, you will have opportunity to talk about thanking God for food in our homes. Sometimes you will sing an appropriate song, make a comment about the activity, or use a Bible verse to fit a natural home situation. Let the children enjoy "free," unstructured play much of the time, but be at hand to enter the situation when you have an opportunity to direct their thinking to the Lord.

The music center

The music center will not be used every week, but it is a good place to introduce new songs and provide the children with an opportunity to enjoy music. You may use a record player and the records recommended in your curriculum. Some of these will be activity records, giving the children an opportunity to move to music. Preschoolers will not sit quietly merely listening to music without words. The music center may also be a good place to learn new finger plays and review old ones. Four- and five-year-olds will enjoy singing familiar songs to a guitar or autoharp accompaniment. Sometimes children at this center will learn a song to sing during the large group time. This center also provides opportunity for children to experiment with rhythm band instruments.

The book center

Your book center will be some open shelves or perhaps a table where books are displayed. Any book chosen for this center should be judged for its teaching value. The books need not be confined to Bible stories, but they should stimulate children to develop spiritually and emotionally. Books on special subjects are always available. Consult with your Christian bookstore about books that help preschoolers, such as books that develop attitudes about God's good gifts. *How God Gives Us Apples* and *Growing-up!* are two good examples of books for preschoolers. While you will want many books in your department, display only a few at a time. Plan to have one book for each child who comes to this center. Be ready to look at a book with several children, remembering that two- and three-year-olds will not be patient if you read extensively. Merely commenting and questioning as you share a book with them will be enough to hold interest and direct their thinking to the Lord. All preschoolers enjoy looking at the same book more than once and hearing the same story again.

The puzzle center

A puzzle center interests all preschoolers. Many good, sturdy wooden puzzles are available. *Never* waste money on flimsy puzzles that do not fit well. Older primaries and juniors may patiently put together tiny pieces or flimsy pieces, but not preschoolers. If you are working with two- and three-year-olds, provide some puzzles with only three or four pieces. Five-year-olds can work puzzles with as many as twenty pieces. Establish some rules at the puzzle center: We do not throw pieces. We work with only one puzzle at a time. We sit far enough away from the next person so that the pieces do not get mixed. We return one puzzle before taking another. If you do not have a puzzle rack, designate a shelf where puzzles are to be kept.

The block center

The block center will be a very popular place with many preschoolers. They need opportunities to construct, to put things together, and to build. A toddler needs sturdy, lightweight cardboard blocks, but you will want to supply wooden blocks for three-, four-, and five-year-olds. Hollow wooden blocks are useful because they come in big sizes and can be used to build things a child can use—steps, a wall, a train or a boat. Hardwood blocks are expensive, but they are durable and safe. They will last many years with good care and occasional refinishing.

The centers described thus far will be used as beginning

activities. Sometimes they may be used to reinforce the lesson. The children may build a city wall with the blocks *after* the Bible story. They may look at a book as part of the lesson application, or they may go to the nature center to develop appreciation for God's creation after a large-group activity. However, these uses of the learning centers are the exception, not the rule.

The art center

Art center activities, on the other hand, are often used as an expressional activity, encouraging the children to express what they have learned. Some curriculums will offer art as one of several activities to use in helping children to show how they applied the lesson. However, another course of study may suggest the same art activity for all children in the small groups. Still other curriculums may consider "art" the printed handwork project which a child completes according to directions.

You will want to vary materials and methods at the art center. Do not think of crayons as the only medium for preschoolers, but experiment with clay, paint, chalk, and freehand cutting and pasting.

Do not be discouraged if your children are hesitant to use some art materials. If they have not used the material before, they may very well be hesitant. Talk with them about the material and demonstrate how to use it. If a child asks you to draw something for him, talk with him about the object. "What color is your house? What color of dog are you thinking about? Where do you think the wheels on the truck belong?" Do not draw for the child, because you will deny him the joy of personal achievement. Do not go over a child's work to show him what he should have done. You are not teaching art; you are using art to help a child express what he has learned.

Crayons

With kindergarten crayons (largest size available) and large sheets of paper, two-year-olds can color freely. Newsprint or smooth sheets of wrapping paper will be satisfactory. The children may work at a table, on the floor, or draw on paper fastened on a wall.

How does a child move from mere motion to meaning? At first the young child seems to attack the paper with his crayon, holding the crayon in a tight grip to make uncontrolled lines we call scribbles. Later the child uses the crayon in almost a rhythmic motion, repeating the same design, but using a variety of colors.

As the child matures physically and mentally, he will have better control over the crayon. He begins to give his pictures names, and his art may have recognizable meaning. We may be able to see this stage in the work of some three-year-olds, most four-year-olds, and all five-year-olds. When children are about four, they begin to be selective in colors and prefer to draw something that has meaning for them. Notice that colors have meaning for children, but they may not be the traditional meanings. Some four-year-olds were drawing "big" things God made. There was joy and ecstasy on her face as Frannie drew a purple maple. Terry chose pink for his elm tree. (If you decide that only particular colors should be used in a handwork project, put out only those colors. Do not try to persuade the children to choose only the colors you suggest.)

Once a child is capable of recognizable pictures, he will grow in his ability to portray ideas. He will draw things as they appear to him, sometimes including not only what he sees but what he knows should be in the picture. He may draw the interior of a house and try to include all the furniture. Usually the object that is most important to the child will be the largest. You may, for example, see very small shepherds worshiping a "large" baby Jesus.

Clay

Clay is a good medium for young children because it does not require coordination of the smaller muscles and because they will enjoy pounding, punching, thumping, rolling, and pulling it. You will seldom use clay for a take-home project, but this medium provides ample opportunity for expression.

Do not expect the children to make something immediately. The first stages of clay work are handling and experimenting. You may need to show children how to make a shape or develop a form. Once the children have seen your work and understand it, roll the clay back into a ball because you do not want to stifle creativity or invite frustration by providing a model.

When you make clay available, provide twelve-inch square boards, such as corrugated cardboard, to use on a newspaper-covered table. Then you must also provide clean-up facilities. If you have only a few children working with clay, a nearby washroom will be adequate. However, if more than six children are using clay, you may want to invest in some of the premoistened tissues now available.

You will find a variety of clays or play doughs on the market, or you may make your own flour- and salt-clay. Even though the dough or clay keeps for some time in airtight containers, do not use it too long, because it picks up dirt and germs. Vary the color of the clay, but explain that colors are not to be mixed. Do not expect a child to mold recognizable objects. Some children may, but others will not succeed in making an object that you can identify. For this reason, many teachers consider clay one of the least valuable activities.

Paint

Using paints will make more work for you, teacher, but the children will enjoy this new medium and profit from it. You will not want to use painting every Sunday, but you may offer several opportunities during the year to do finger painting, spatter painting, easel painting, or print making.

Print making may provide a new experience for many of your preschoolers. In print making, the child presses an object into tempera paint and then onto a sheet of paper. The object may be a bottle cap, a bit of sponge, a napkin ring, and so on. Unless you demonstrate more than once, children doing print making for the first time have a tendency to use the object as they would a brush, scrubbing back and forth in an attempt to cover the paper. These children are not stupid; they are merely trying to use a new object in an old way.

Painting requires adequate preparation, including telling parents that children will be painting in Sunday school. If parents know you plan to use this medium, they will dress their children in washable clothing. Parents can also supply smocks or aprons for their children. You must have adequate clean-up facilities for painting—a nearby washroom or a large basin of water and towels.

Spatter painting is not as creative as easel painting, but it is easier to prepare for and supervise. You will need paper, a square or rectangular wooden frame covered with a piece of screening, tempera paint, and a toothbrush. The child pins a pattern, that you have prepared ahead of time, to a sheet of construction paper. Then he places the frame over the pattern or object, and the brush is dipped into the paint and rubbed over the screen. You then lift off the screen and allow the painting to dry with the pattern still pinned in place. After the paint has dried, lift the object or pattern from the paper, and the outline of a silhouette is left on the paper.

Finger painting offers freedom of expression, because the child does not have to manipulate any tools. It is an activity for groups of not more than four children. Finger paint is available commercially, or you may find a recipe in a craft book and make your own starch-based paint.

Selection of paper for finger painting is very important. It must be a glossy, nonabsorbent paper, such as shelf paper.

The paper is prepared by either dipping it into a pan of water or wetting it with a sponge. Then about a teaspoonful of paint is placed in the middle of the paper. The child uses his hands to spread the paint over the entire surface. Children finger paint feelings more often than events. After the children have heard the Bible story of Jesus stilling the storm, they may paint the waves—high and fierce at first and then calm and smooth. You may leave the papers to dry on the tabletop or floor, but they will dry more quickly if you can suspend them from a clothesline.

Easel painting requires a homemade or purchased easel, large brushes (bristles of 1" to 1½" wide), and tempera paint. Newsprint or wrapping paper works well. Spread newspapers under the easel. If you have a double easel, two children can paint at the same time. You will need to show the children how to use one color at a time, with a different brush for each color. Demonstrate how the child is to dip the brush into the container, press it against the side to remove excess paint, and then move it across the paper. The child soon learns that dipping his brush into the paint frequently is better than scrubbing.

Preschoolers should never be asked to paint with the small brushes and boxes of paint used by elementary pupils. The types of painting described here are the methods that preschoolers can use satisfactorily.

Though painting is a valuable learning activity, you will want to evaluate its use for your children. Use the questions given in the first section of this chapter to help you evaluate its use in your situation. Then be sure that you have time, space, smocks, understanding parents, and the materials for painting. Finger painting and easel painting may not be activities for you. However, most preschool departments can manage spatter painting and print making.

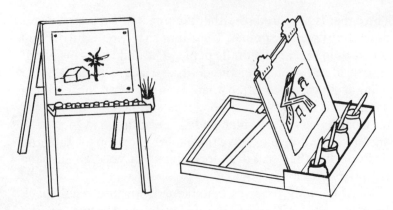

Fig. 3. Double and tabletop easels.

Cutting and pasting

Preschool children cannot cut out small figures, but four-and five-year-olds can try tearing shapes, such as leaves to add to trees, or flowers for a garden. When you are teaching a child to cut, draw straight lines for cutting, then circles, and then more difficult outlines. Do not criticize a child if he does not cut on the lines; leave this for the public school teacher to perfect. But do provide preschoolers with scissors that have round safety ends, not the sharp-pointed ones the children will choose if given a choice. Do not waste money on plastic scissors, because they will not cut paper. Always test scissors before you purchase them.

Preschoolers from age three on will enjoy pasting. The younger children are not ready for cutting, but they can paste in place what you provide. It will take time for a three-year-old to learn that he needs only a small dab of paste. Be patient with him till he discovers this.

Any art activity should be the child's own work. If you have to do most of the work on a project, it is too difficult for preschoolers and is not a good learning experience for them. Remember that when a young child paints a picture, draws with crayons, or makes a clay object, he is not creating art.

He is setting down his impressions. Because preschoolers cannot write and many are still struggling to verbalize, encourage art as a means of expressing what they have learned or how they feel as a result of what you have taught.

Whatever expressional activities you provide, be sure they are meaningful to the children. Sometimes playing out the story is the most meaningful. Do not assume that an activity will be meaningful unless you make it so. Too often children leave Sunday school with a take-home project that means nothing to them. Do not let children lose the meaning through the fun of doing. Talk about the purpose of the project and review it again before the child takes it home.

REACT

1. Do you agree that preschoolers need both large and small group activities? Why? Does your answer include the fact that preschoolers learn through their senses?
2. If communicating God's Word to little children is important, are small group activities too great an effort for you to undertake? Why not?

ACT

1. What interest or learning centers are you using now?
2. What centers are suggested in your curriculum? Remember, if the activities are suggested without being set up at a center, the curriculum is recognizing and advising the small group learning activities.
3. If the learning centers or activities themselves are not suggested in your curriculum, what should you do?
4. If you have not been using the learning activities described in this chapter, which one are you planning to try first? Try it soon!

8

Where Will
You Teach?

We know that children learn better and are happier in an accepting and caring environment. You could follow every suggestion in this chapter for rooms and materials but not provide the caring, loving environment that will help children love God and His Word. *You* make the difference! Strive for the best facilities, materials, and methods, but do not lose sight of the fact that the children will learn most from you and your relationship to the Lord. This is something preschoolers can see, hear, and feel emotionally.

Now that you know more about the people you are to teach and how you are to teach them, you are ready to think about where you will teach. What is an ideal room for preschoolers? How can you adapt to a less-than-ideal situation? How big a room do you need? What is the best shape for a room? What should be in a room for preschoolers? Is it possible to have either too much or too little furniture? How many children belong in one room?

First, take a look at your preschool departments. Ideally you will have a separate room for two-year olds, for three-year-olds, and perhaps one room for four- and five-year-olds. Ideally, a good room for two-year-olds will have thirty-five square feet of space for each child. This is child space. It does not include the space occupied by storage areas or large equipment. About fifteen three-year-olds may be grouped in one room—no more than ten or twelve two-year-olds in one room. Use the same space allotment for three-year-olds. Four- and five-year-olds may be in separate rooms or in one room. Limit the group to no more than twenty or twenty-five children and provide thirty square feet of space for each child. These figures express the ideal, of course, but they will give you a standard to work toward.

If you were to plan the ideal arrangement, you would provide a separate room for each age. The rooms would be slightly more rectangular than square in shape, because such floor space is more adaptable to arranging and rearranging interest centers, play space, and an area for all the children to gather together for the Bible story and worship activities. However, if you do not have the ideal situation, keep adapting the space you have to create the best possible environment for preschoolers. Keep the requirements for good rooms before you and continue to make as many adaptations, changes, and improvements as possible. If you cannot do everything this year, set up a five-year improvement program. Check your rooms against the following list.

1. All preschool rooms should be on the ground level, not in the basement!
2. Provide floor coverings that are smooth, durable, and easily cleaned.
3. Be sure that all window and door areas are completely safe.
4. Cover any hot pipes and radiators in your room. You should also insert protective coverings over all low electrical outlets. An outlet may challenge some child to try inserting the tip of a scissor or some other metal object.
5. Provide adequate heat and light.
6. Keep the room clean. Remember preschoolers are the people who spend more time on the floor than any other age group in your Sunday school.
7. Paint the room a color that appeals to children, not, for example, a gray-green that is calming to adults.
8. Remove any broken furniture, accumulation of unused materials such as hymnbooks, old visual-aid equipment, or out-of-season decorations.

If you really want to evaluate a preschool room, take time to remove all the furniture. Now take a look at the room, the windows, the walls, and the floor covering. Before replacing anything, decide what you like and do not like about the room. Will a fresh coat of paint help? New curtains? A different floor covering? What can you afford to do first?

Take one more look at the walls before you replace any of the furniture. What is on them? Are there pictures that appeal to children? Pictures, bulletin boards, coat hooks, a picture rail—anything children need to see or use—should be at a child's eye-level. Don't guess about a child's eye level, but plan to measure the exact height the next time you have one of the children in the room. If children are to learn, the environment must help them.

Now begin replacing the furniture, evaluating each piece. Do not return any piece unless it serves a purpose. A preschool room is not the place for cast-off furniture. Chairs and tables are important. The chairs should have seats ten or twelve inches from the floor. (Use the smaller chairs for two- and three-year-olds.) A good table will be sturdy, have an easily cleaned surface, and measure ten inches higher than the seats of the chairs used at the table. If you do not have space for both tables and chairs, sacrifice the chairs, because your preschoolers will not mind standing as they work at the tables.

Where are the shelves that children can use for storing materials? (You will want high shelves with locked doors for your materials.) Do you have adequate shelving for books, puzzles, and toys? Where are the blocks stored? Shelves are good storage space for the large hollow wooden blocks or for the lightweight cardboard blocks. A box is the best place for smaller wooden blocks.

Arrange your rooms so that they do not look cluttered. If possible, use a nearby hallway or room for the children's coatroom. Parents can help children there, leaving more space in your room. You may cut the door to your room in half horizontally so that both halves open and close independently of each other. This type of door is often called a dutch door. You will open the top of the door to deliver a two- or three-year-old to his parents, who will take him to the outdoor wrap area.

After you have provided for the essentials, you are ready to add other items that make the environment more pleasant, but be sure you have room for them. Additional items for the learning centers are described in chapter 7. A piano, coat rack for adults, rack for drying finger paintings, an adult rocker or desk would be welcome additions to your room if you have the space. Perhaps you feel that a piano is essential. It is a good piece of equipment, but preschoolers will sing just as well without accompaniment or with an autoharp or guitar. You set the stage for a good learning experience when you carefully plan for the equipment that meets the needs of your pupils. Unless children are going to make use of the equipment, is it worth having in the room?

All preschool workers want to achieve the ideal, but few will. Probably the most important need for your children is space—to move, to play out stories, and to learn through activities. But even if your space is limited, remember that you are the one who can help the children learn. Plan for improved conditions in the future, but realize that you set the atmosphere for learning by the interesting things you have in the room and the varied activities you plan for the children.

Learning materials

Because children learn through doing—involving touching, seeing, and hearing—there should be plenty of materials for them to use. Provide pictures, puppets, objects and models, flannelboards and figures for them, flash cards, dioramas, flip charts, peep boxes, bulletin boards, and all of the materials used in the small group activities or interest centers described in chapter 7. Your curriculum materials will help you learn about many of these teaching aids. Some of them are available from your Christian bookstore or Sunday school supplier, and others you will want to make yourself.

Pictures help enrich the experiences of all children. They are a valuable resource. Prepared picture sets are often a part of curriculum materials, but you will also want to collect other pictures from magazines, newspapers, display materials, catalogs, calendars, church literature, discarded picture books, and school supply houses.

Why are pictures important? Here are some ideas adapted from the book, *Guiding Preschoolers* by Florence Hearn.[1]

1. Pictures can be touched and handled!

---

1. Florence Hearn, *Guiding Preschoolers* (Nashville: Convention Press, 1969), p. 83. Used by permission.

2. Pictures provide information that children cannot get otherwise.
3. Pictures help to correct wrong ideas and serve to reinforce experiences children have had.
4. Pictures enrich a storytelling experience or a conversation which children have had.
5. Pictures stimulate interest and encourage children to develop their imaginations.
6. Pictures can help create an atmosphere in which young children can communicate with God.
7. Pictures enrich, explain, and motivate children to become familiar with Bible thoughts and verses.
8. Pictures can be used to stimulate conversation and to assist in decision-making.

Here are some guidelines to follow in selecting pictures. Use good quality, clear, large pictures with few details. Show a picture of one elephant, for example, rather than a herd of them. Trim the picture carefully and mount it on a harmonizing shade of construction paper and then on poster board or cardboard. Investigate some of the newer processes available to you through art stores, such as laminating a picture that will be handled frequently or dry mounting pictures for a longer-lasting adhesive process. When you use a picture, be sure that all the children can see it, even if this means taking turns. Preschoolers will enjoy pictures that have people in them.

It is impossible to list all of the teaching aids available to you, but here are some of the most worthwhile:

Flannelboards may be homemade or purchased. You can buy flannelboard figures or make your own figures to illustrate the Bible story. Preschoolers will be happy with simple chenille-wire figures, or you may find figures in old Sunday school papers or Bible coloring books. Try to have all figures for one story in proportion to one another. Paste scraps of felt, suede, flannel, or sandpaper to the backs of the figures.

Flip charts are made from chart paper or lightweight

cardboard. Use one picture on a sheet to illustrate one idea in a Bible verse or song. Most preschoolers cannot read, so you need not include any words.

Puppets deserve an entire book. They are good to use in telling a story, or the puppets may act out the story. A puppet may encourage children to put away supplies or come to the Bible story area. Investigate available puppets and check to see how your curriculum recommends using them.

Bulletin boards are used to display pictures, seasonal objects, children's art, and teaching exhibits. *Preschool Bulletin Boards,* written by Mary E. LeBar and published by Scripture Press Publications (1965), is especially good.

Dioramas are best suited to older preschoolers, because the figures are small and the scenes may be complicated. A diorama is a three-dimensional scene placed in a box that is set on its side. The figures, cut from pictures, are mounted to stand in front of the background.

Peep boxes, usually shoe boxes, are similar to dioramas but are viewed through a peep hole in the end of the box.

Fig. 4. Diorama and peep box.

Your children will want to touch any of the objects that you bring. Touching is a way of learning for the preschooler, therefore do not take objects or pictures to Sunday school unless you expect the children to handle them.

Is yours a balanced program?

Now that you have read about the parts of the Sunday school hour—the teaching methods used most often, and the room, furnishings, and atmosphere—you can better evaluate your program. Is your whole hour meeting the children's needs, or the teachers' convenience? Every preschool teacher is constantly striving to keep things in balance—large and small group activities; quiet and active times; listening and doing—and to reinforce the familiar while introducing new concepts. No two sessions will be exactly alike, but there will be planned variety. You are never engaged in activity for the sake of activity, but you are constantly teaching new words and ideas, and giving new experiences to your children.

Teaching preschoolers is work, but it is worth all the effort you put into it. Remember, yours is a rare privilege—the opportunity of teaching young children about the Lord and leading them to love Him and serve Him.

REACT

1. How many opportunities are there in the average Sunday school session for a child to worship? For example, a child is watching the rain beat against the windowpane, and you say, "Thank You, God, for rain, which makes things grow." How many opportunities for worship are you using?

2. If you are going to teach children through their senses—not just their listening ears—you will spend many hours searching for the materials you need. Is this worth the time?

ACT

1. If you are a wise teacher, you will plan ahead. Go through your manual when you first receive it. Note the Bible content, planning to study it in your own personal devo-

tions. Then make a list of the materials you will want to collect and use: nature objects, pictures, items for a tabletop scene, etc.

2. Prepare ahead of time. You may cut, color, and assemble some materials in the moments when you are waiting for someone or relaxing at home. Try it.

3. Involve others in helping you. Preschool teachers probably need more materials than any other teachers in the Sunday school. Ask senior citizens to cut and mount pictures for you. Invite teenagers to sort papers, prepare bulletin boards, or help in other ways.

Make a list of the jobs that someone else could do to help you prepare learning materials. Now pray that the Lord will lead you to the person who can be your helper behind the scenes.

9

How Does the Staff Work Together?

"Serve one another with the particular gifts
God has given each of you, as faithful
dispensers of the magnificently varied grace of
God" (1 Pe 4:10, Phillips).

Teaching preschoolers is a team ministry. As a teaching team, members of a preschool department staff use a variety of skills, and in a variety of ways they are dispensers of God's wonderfully varied grace. On other, older age levels, teaching may be a transaction involving one teacher with a small class of learners. For many reasons, this is neither effective nor desirable with preschoolers.

Often preschoolers require individual attention. An accident happens; a child becomes upset and strikes out; one is overcome with sudden homesickness and needs comforting. Many such incidents make it important that enough staff members be present to show the personal attention so important to giving younger children a sense of warmth and security.

But preschool staff members are teachers as well as comforters. The individualized, interest-center teaching and the conversational teaching approach that fill play activities with meaning, mean that enough staff members are needed to relate to little clusters of children. This informal time is prime teaching time and demands staff members who are trained and who have a thorough understanding of the ways preschoolers are to be taught and the ways they learn.

Perhaps even more important, however, is that each preschool staff member adds something of the warmth of his own personality to the learning experience. *Who we are* as persons who love Jesus and who love the children does come through to children. As they learn to trust their teachers and sense the security of their love, this attitude of trust and security helps provide the foundations of a growing faith in Christ discussed in chapters one and two.

What's important in helping a staff become a team, a *team* that teaches, rather than simply a group of individuals who teach?

Staff roles

A variety of roles are important in the department team,

and can be filled by one or several of the staff. Each teacher, of course, is first of all a friend who has concern for each child and finds opportunity to show it, from the first step into the room, on through individualized and group activities, to the final warm good-bye at the end of the hour. Each teacher on the preschool staff needs to relate to the children as individual personalities; relating to them in a group is far less important at this early age.

Each teacher also will be called on for conversational teaching at the interest and activity centers. This means each will need to know how to use play as a teaching medium (rather than simply supervising free play). It also means that each teacher will need to understand thoroughly the content and teaching strategy of each class hour. It's not enough for only the department superintendent or master teacher to tell the Bible story and for the rest of the staff simply to be there to supervise the children. As we've seen, every part of the preschool class hour is a teaching activity. Songs, prayer, and play are as much part of the Bible teaching impact of preschool ministry as the story itself.

While each staff member does have teaching ministry roles, there are additional special roles that need to be filled. "Story lady" (or—increasingly—man!) is an important one. The storyteller needs to understand preschooler's short attention span, tell the story with warmth and interest, and use the many aids that can help make Bible story time a fascinating one for tots.

One of the staff can also take responsibility for songs during worship time, or—in the case of two- and three-year-olds—each teacher should be ready to sing the simple, repetitive teaching songs that come with good curriculums.

The division of labor made possible by the variety of roles in teaching preschoolers means that individuals with special talents and skills can use them to make unique contributions. The best storyteller on the team can accept this special role; special talents in preparation of interest center or other projects can be utilized. Grandparents and dads fit into and make distinctive contributions to the teaching team.

It is important then to always think of the department staff as a team, not as separate and individual teachers. And it's important to take definite steps to make sure that the staff functions as a team!

Unified understanding

What elements go into building a staff into a team? One of the most important is a common purpose and understanding of preschool ministry. The issues focused on in this book —goals in teaching, objectives, how preschoolers learn, impact of various teaching methods, structure of the hour and the room—are all important foundations of effective team performance.

However, within the framework provided by general principles, many specific and shared plans need to be developed. All on the teaching team need to understand the goals of the unit and the weekly individual lessons. The team should talk over the needs of individuals in their department and plan ways to use the curriculum objectives to meet specific needs. Interest centers should be discussed and planned by the team, with each individual understanding how each play activity contributes toward reaching the objectives of the session and unit. Teaching songs correlated with the unit should be learned by all as well. Often special decorations for the room, or special activity projects suggested in the curriculum, will need to be planned for.

This kind of coordination demands that the team hold regular planning meetings. While normally these will not be needed weekly, each new unit of lessons clearly demands a staff get-together.

What happens when a staff gets together to plan for a coming unit? Here's an outline of a possible approach to such a meeting.

Unit Planning Meeting

7:30—7:50	Sharing, evaluation of last unit Emphasis on growth of individuals observed
7:50—8:10	Preview of Bible content, goals, and objectives of upcoming unit and individual lessons (by superintendent or storyteller)
8:10—8:40	Preview of suggested interest center or play-learning activities. Generation of additional ideas, modifications in view of department resources, space, etc.
8:40—8:50	Learning of correlated songs
8:50—9:00	Planning of special roles or tasks.
9:00—9:30	Discussion of special needs of individual children, especially in view of upcoming unit. Prayer for the children about the truths being taught.

This kind of planning meeting will be most meaningful if each of the staff has his own teacher's manual and studies it before the meeting. It will also be helpful if the superintendent will have prepared for each teacher a statement of unit and lesson objectives and ties these in with the overall goals specified in chapter 4 of this book.

While the unit planning meeting is a very important gathering for the staff, other kinds of staff meetings are also important. If a unit of lessons extends beyond four weeks, to six or seven weeks, an evaluation session in the middle of the unit would be important. These midunit meetings give opportunity for exploring different areas of the department's ministry as well as the practical, day-to-day operation of the team. Here's a typical midunit meeting outline. Notice that it stresses staff sharing and problem solving and focusing on the individual children in the department.

Midunit Planning Meeting

7:30—8:00	Sharing, evaluation of progress in unit Discussion of problems, plans for solution

8:00—8:20   Discussion of individual children
              Development of a staff anecdotal record
              (each individual contributes observations, in-
              formation on each child, to build together a
              better understanding of deeper concern for
              him)

8:20—9:20   Special project study

9:20—9:30   Prayer time

What might a "special project" be? Anything dealing with
the general effectiveness of the department's ministry. For
instance, you might work together on a plan for visiting the
families, providing a resource sheet to help parents continue
your teaching thrust at home. Or you might work on decorat-
ing your room or preparing some special object for an interest center. Or you might have a report on a book on
teaching preschoolers. You might view a film or have a
preschool teacher from the public school talk about discipline problems and how to handle them effectively.

Actually, your special projects studies will grow out of the
needs you and the staff observe in your local situation. If
regular staff meetings are a feature of your preschool ministry, you'll find a growing number of areas become "special
interest" concerns of your staff! And you'll need time like
this to deal with them.

The point we've been making is clear. Teaching preschoolers is a *team* affair. And regular staff get-togethers are
utterly necessary if the staff members are to grow into a
functioning teaching team. To the extent that all your staff
members share a common philosophy of teaching and learning and work together to plan and carry out unit and weekly
programs, a team spirit will be developed. Developing the
staff into a team may take many months. But this concern is a
priority for those seeking to have a quality ministry with the
young children who are invited to come to Jesus.

Common spiritual concern

There's more to staff meetings than program planning and more to team effectiveness than individual teaching skills. A common spiritual concern, a unity of spirit, a fellowship of love on the team, are vital ingredients of every Christian relationship, and especially of the relationship of those engaged in a common ministry.

The spiritual dimension is demonstrated in two areas, both of which emphasize Jesus' own concern for persons: a team with a common spiritual concern has learned, first, to care about each other and, second, to care about the children as individuals.

Staff times together need to reflect growing concern of the members for each other. Note that in the meeting plans, time is always given for sharing. If anything, the suggested times for this vital interaction are too short! In many churches, fellowship or sharing time precedes the planning meetings. A meal together in one of the homes; a time for studying Scripture together; time to pray with and for each other —these are all important dimensions of the staff's team life.

Particularly when a staff is just forming, special times to get to know one another are important. The deepening of prayer fellowship over the months of shared ministry will bring constantly greater depth to the relationship—and to the ministry.

Getting to know the children as individual personalities is another vital aspect of developing spiritual concern. Our ministry of teaching is a ministry to individuals, each of whom is important and precious to God. We come to appreciate the importance of each and share increasingly in God's love for each individual by coming to know each one better.

One way to increase knowing is by keeping team or staff anecdotal records. Each time you get together as a staff, spend some time discussing individual preschoolers. Share what each of the staff has observed during class. If you've been in the home or know the home, add to your record home background information. These records are kept to enable you to see progress as each child develops through his year(s) with the department, and they help staff members see each child as a unique individual. Prayer for the children as individuals and for special needs they may have will further deepen the spiritual concern that marks teachers who share Christ's love for the young.

Sometimes pairing of staff members into visitation teams can serve a dual purpose of helping the staff come to know each other better and get a better insight into individuals and their families. Whenever there are special tasks to accomplish, if two or more of the staff can be asked to work together, you'll increase the opportunity for staff involvement with each other in a spiritually significant way.

In everything, be sensitive to the personal dimensions of your ministry, the personal relationships within the staff and the personal concern for preschoolers that will grow as each child is increasingly seen as an individual to be loved for himself and led to trust and know both the adults who make up your staff and the Lord you represent.

REACT

1. In what ways does your present staff function as a team? In what ways does it need to grow in its team unity?
2. Beside the name of each teacher in your department, list his special abilities or talents. How does he fit into the team? What abilities could be better utilized?

ACT

1. Schedule a team unit-planning meeting for the next unit, and work through with the other staff members just what you'll want to accomplish then.
2. Begin department anecdotal records on each child in your department.

10

How Can We Help Parents?

"And these words, which I command thee this day, shall be in thine heart: and thou shalt teach them diligently unto thy children, and shalt talk of them when thou sittest in thine house, and when thou walkest by the way, and when thou liest down, and when thou risest up" (Deu 6:6-7).

The primary communicators of faith to preschoolers are their parents. This is God's order, and it has never been superceded.

This does not, of course, reduce the importance of the church's ministry to preschoolers. Instead it establishes the church's ministry as an adjunct and supplement to the home, not as a substitute or supplanter. At the same time, it increases the importance of the church's preschool ministry by showing the potential for extending that ministry through the week by aiding parents in their teaching tasks!

When we think about helping parents teach preschoolers, we need to do several things. We need to review the nature of teaching as it applies to preschoolers. We need to look at the problems facing parents. And we need to realize the resources we can provide to parents.

First, as discussed in earlier chapters, we need to remember that teaching preschoolers is a part of nurture. The word *nurture* implies growth, development. It speaks of a process, not of a product. No ministry to preschoolers can, in itself, produce spiritually mature adults. The capacity for maturity—be it physical, social, emotional, or spiritual —awaits growth into adulthood. So our teaching of preschoolers is not focused on the product. It is focused on supplying what is needed for the *process of growth to proceed normally and healthily.*

In earlier chapters, we've seen that preschoolers need a relational context in which they feel loved and secure if they are to grow as open, trusting persons. We've seen some of the basic Bible concepts they need to build into their understanding of life and reality: truths about who God and Jesus are, and that the Bible is God's Book. We've also seen some of the simple attitudes and behaviors we want to foster, encouraging them at the earliest ages to begin responding to God with loving obedience.

It is very important to realize that such learning involves not merely information but *being*. Jesus told His followers,

"A disciple when he is fully taught will *be like* his teacher" (Lk 6:40). *Being* is the focus of Christian teaching, and children learn and become like their teachers. A primary focus, then, of ministry to preschoolers is on providing relationships for them with adults who do love and obey God, and who will be the right kind of models for these littlest disciples.

As a teacher ministering in Sunday school or children's church, you are a model for the preschoolers you teach. But the *primary model* remains their parents: the adults with whom they spend most of their waking hours.

What do parents need to be good models for their preschoolers? Deuteronomy 6 points out that the parents need to take God's Word to heart, to make it a living part of their own lives and personalities. Then they need to talk about God and His words in the process of daily living. The truths on adults' hearts need to be shared with their children. What is important, then, is not that the parents know everything about the Bible or try to teach everything about the Bible at home but that they grow in their relationship with Jesus; that they demonstrate His love and trustworthiness in their family; that, as they live daily with their children, they talk about God and His place in the family's life. This simple pattern of *lived faith* is critical during the early years of a child's life: it lays the foundation for his future life with God and with other people.

Parents need to understand preschool teaching as *being* and build into their lives ways and times to express their faith in simple, meaningful ways.

This brief insight into home training of preschoolers helps us understand many of the problems facing parents. Most problems hinge on a failure to grasp the developmental nature of preschoolers' nurture and a lack of information as to how parents can make the most significant contributions to their tots' spiritual growth. We often have teacher-training emphases, but parent training has historically been neglected by the church. Noting this, we can see one immediate answer to the question of how we can help parents. We can help parents by getting them to better understand their teaching ministry! Chapters in this book that are particularly applicable are the first, fourth, fifth, and seventh. Insights given here into preschool ministry are just those that parents (as well as church staff teachers) need to know!

But how do we help parents better understand the nature of their nurturing ministry with preschoolers?

1. We might invite small groups of parents to meet in different teachers' homes for "insight" sessions.
2. We might encourage parents to read books like this one and *You, the Parent*, the Effective Teaching book specially written for them.
3. We might develop and send home monthly newsletters, using excerpts from this and similar books as part of the content.
4. We might divide the families between staff members, and have teams of two teachers each visit the homes to explain the department's goals and philosophy.
5. We might encourage a mother's club for sharing ideas and talking over common problems and concerns.
6. We might encourage parents to visit Sunday school for several consecutive Sundays, limiting the number present to no more than two couples.

Each of these approaches is a costly one in terms of time and effort. It involves asking a staff to go the second mile (and even a third!) in an already demanding ministry. But this kind of ministry *to the home* is of vital importance to the future of the children you have come to know and care for.

It is true, of course, that the most basic needs of the home, for parents to be growing Christians, probably cannot be met by the preschool staff. Parents will need to be involved with other ministries of the church—adult classes, the worship services, perhaps small home Bible study and prayer groups—as a source for their own feeding and development. Yet the friendship and encouragement of staff members as other adults can provide a source of mutual fellowship and encouragement.

Contact with the home is particularly needed if the parents are not yet Christians. When visiting a non-Christian home, it's important that you approach contacts with a clear vision of your purpose. While your long-range goal is to draw the adults to Christ and thus lay the foundation for a truly Christian home, a direct, or "hard sell," evangelism is seldom best. Non-Christians need not only to hear the Gospel presented, they need to see the reality of Jesus in His disciples! To build a relationship with non-Christians in which the reality of Jesus is communicated, you must assume that they are interested (with you) in the spiritual growth of their children. (After all, they are bringing or permitting their children to be in your department!) You also need to realize that God loves them *as they are*, and that it is your place to love them as He does (cf. Mt 5:43-48). As they come to feel confident in your love and concern for them, their defenses will be lowered, and they will be open to exploring Jesus' claims. This "gentle evangelism" approach will not, of course, be one you will take in every situation. Meeting a passing stranger, there is hardly time for development of a relationship. Then, if God leads, a direct presentation of the Gospel is fitting. But when you have built-in points of continuing contact, as through a child in your department, the gentle approach is nearly always the right one. As you express Jesus' love for parents and child, doors will open to share Jesus Himself, and hearts will be readied for that message.

Thus far, then, we've noted two needs of the home and ways that the preschool staff can be used by God to minister to them. Christian nurture demands Christians! And God can use you to build relationships with adults through which they may be led to Christ and their growth encouraged. While evangelism and nurture of adults may not be the primary responsibility of the preschool staff, each contribution in these areas is vital to the overall development of the children you teach. Second, parents do need to understand the principles of nurture on which preschool ministry is based. This educational task *is* a primary responsibility of preschool departments. Understanding the nature of preschool ministry better than any other group in the church, you will want to share your understanding with moms and dads.

There is another important way you can help parents. Not only can you help them grasp principles: you can provide resources to enrich home teaching! Actually, these resources are the very ones you develop for your in-class teaching.

1. Bible story pictures can be pinned next to a child's bed for nighttime conversation and reminders.
2. The simple teaching songs used in church can be supplied to parents, to be sung with the children during the week.
3. The take-home papers provided with most curriculums can be read and talked about in the home.
4. Interest center activities, involving the children in play that uses many of the senses, can be communicated to parents as units are launched. Parents can be shown how to involve their children in similar play at home and how to teach them conversationally.
5. A bulletin board in the kitchen or art projects taped to the refrigerator can be suggested to hold Sunday or at-home handwork creations.
6. Study of a unit of preschool lessons will usually suggest several things parents might do at home that have relation to what is being taught: a nature walk outside, a visit to the store or zoo. These and many other simple activities

can be done together, with spontaneous moments for prayer or worship or talking about God.

7. The child's memory verse, added to other verses the family might be learning, can be repeated nightly at the supper table.
8. Simple books from the church library or a local Christian bookstore can be recommended and used.
9. "Make-it" projects (such as a collage) that Mom and child do together can be suggested.

This ministry of providing resources is a very practical and very powerful ministry for enriching the home life of your preschoolers. And there are a number of avenues through which to communicate these resources. There are home visits, parent visits and observations of class, and weekly take-home papers for the children. There are newsletters that can be mailed, spontaneous contacts that can be made with mothers while shopping, mothers' club meetings, and so on.

Of these, probably the newsletter is one of the most powerful yet easiest to do. All it takes is an editor (one of your department staff or a special recruit to major in home-ministry coordination) and a little effort.

What might go into such a newsletter? When should it be mailed? Normally, a newsletter might be sent at the beginning of each unit of lessons. For extra long units, it could be distributed monthly. Typical contents might be:

1. A statement of unit and lesson aims as developed in the unit planning meeting (see chap. 9). Included here should also be the Bible passages used.
2. A column of "things to do" with the children at home to reinforce the teaching. Interest-center activities can be described (with conversational teaching hints) as they are in your curriculum.

3. Songs used with the unit (including the tunes) are another possible feature.
4. A book report, highlighting a specific idea or concept that provides instant help (See Bibliography at the end of this book for possible purchase and review list.)
5. News of children and families. Chatty items, what little Glenna said, a good idea shared at a mothers' club meeting, etc.
6. A short, aimed-at-adults devotional based on the passages to be used with the children.

These and many other features will find their way into department newsletters and build the church and the home together into a coordinated ministry unit.

And this is really what we need. It is not a matter of the church *or* the home in ministry to preschoolers. It is a matter of the church working *with* the home! Two powerful avenues that God has given us to touch young lives for time and eternity, with the gentle, yet lasting mark of Jesus Christ. Either of these avenues is incomplete alone. Young children need to learn at home, from their moms and dads. And young children need to learn with each other, in a setting where other adults model and teach the reality of Jesus and the importance of God's Book. And in each of these settings, home and church, young children deserve the *best* Christian nurture we can provide!

In a very real way, the effectiveness of nurture in both these settings does depend on the preschool staff. Because you are an organized team, trained to understand and minister to these youngest of children, you alone in the church will probably have the expertise to equip moms and dads for their ministries. And as you grow in your understanding of your ministry and in your skill as a team, you will be able to communicate to parents what you know and are learning. Because in your curriculum you have a planned teaching program, you will be able to coordinate the learning in each home. So it *is* up to you to take the lead. It *is* up to you to enrich the home life of your preschoolers, as well as to provide a context for spiritual growth on Sunday mornings.

And how wonderful an opportunity this is! God *is* at work in the lives of even these younger children. The foundations of faith *are* being laid.

May God use you increasingly to provide the firmest of foundations. And to open up the future of these tiny ones to the fullness of His love and transforming power.

REACT

1. How important do you feel the home is in the life of a preschooler? Can you see evidence of its importance in the lives of those you teach now?
2. How many parents of those in your department do you believe are now aware of principles of nurture discussed in this book? How many are using teaching tools to coordinate their ministry at home with what you teach Sundays?

ACT

1. Work as a team to create a parents' newsletter. What items would you want to include? Divide up responsibilities and see how long it takes to develop an issue of this powerful parent aid.
2. Discuss with other members of your preschool staff what goals you want to set for helping parents. What do you see as needs? How might these needs best be met? Write out specific objectives.
3. If you choose, now determine how you will work to reach the objectives you spelled out above. Pray about what God wants you to do together in this vital, yet demanding, dimension of your ministry to preschoolers.

Bibliography

Baker, Katherine R., and Fane, Xenia F. *Understanding and Guiding Young Children,* Englewood Cliffs, N.J.: Prentice-Hall, 1967.

Bartlett, Margaret. *Training for Service in the Preschool Department.* Cincinnati: Standard, 1964.

Beadle, Muriel. *A Child's Mind.* New York: Doubleday, 1970.

Beegle, Shirley. *Bible Story Finger Plays and Action Rhymes.* Cincinnati: Standard, 1964.

Chamberlain, Eugene; Harty, Robert A.; Adams, Saxe. *Pre-Schoolers at Church.* Nashville: Convention, 1969.

Chamberlain, Eugene. *When Can a Child Really Believe?* Nashville: Broadman, 1973.

Dillard, Polly Hargis. *The Church Kindergarten.* Nashville: Broadman, 1958.

Gilliland, Anne Hitchcock. *Understanding Preschoolers.* Nashville: Convention, 1969.

Haystead, Wesley. *Ways to Plan and Organize Your Sunday School: Early Childhood, Birth to Five Years.* Glendale, Calif.: Gospel Light, Regal Books, 1971.

Hearn, Florence C. *Guiding Preschoolers.* Nashville: Convention, 1969.

Heron, Frances D. *Kathy Ann, Kindergartner.* Nashville: Abingdon, 1955.

Hymes, James L., Jr. *The Child Under Six.* Englewood Cliffs, N.J.: Prentice-Hall, 1963.

Jenkins, Gladys G.; Schacter, H.; and Bauer, W. W. *These Are Your Children.* Chicago: Scott, Foresman, 1953.

LeBar, Mary E. *YOU Make the Difference for 4s and 5s.* Wheaton, Ill.: Scripture Press, 1974.

————, *Preschool Bulletin Boards.* Wheaton, Ill.: Scripture Press, 1965.

Mow, Anna B., *Your Child from Birth to Rebirth*. Grand Rapids: Zondervan, 1963.

Nicholson, Dorothy. *Toward Effective Teaching of Young Children*. Anderson, Ind.: Warner, 1970.

Rowen, Dolores. *Ways to Help Them Learn: Early Childhood, Birth to Five Years*. Glendale, Calif.: Gospel Light, Regal Books, 1972.

Scott, Louise B.; May, Marion E.; and Shaw, Mildred S. *Puppets for All Grades*. Danville, N.Y.: Owen, 1960.

Soderholm, Marjorie E. *Understanding the Pupil: Part 1, the Preschool Child*. Grand Rapids: Baker, 1955.

Tobey, Katherine M. *Learning and Teaching Through the Senses*. Philadelphia: Westminster, 1959.

————. *The Church Plans for Kindergarten Children*. Philadelphia: Westminster, 1959.

US Department of Health, Education, Welfare. *Your Child from 1 to 6*. Washington, D.C.: US Government Printing Office, 1962.

Young, Leontine. *Life Among the Giants*. New York: McGraw-Hill, 1965.